FOREST Escape

FOREST Escape
a chosen path

Text Copyright ©2023 by Wendy Nelson
Artwork Copyright ©2023 by Wendy Nelson
Photography Copyright ©2023 by Wendy Nelson

Published by MediaTek Grafx
POB 62, Bonnieville, Kentucky, 42713

ISBN 978-1-0879-5548-3

Design and production by MediaTek Grafx, Bonnieville, Kentucky
Special thanks to Joan Swan for loving review, critique and advice

The Publisher has made every effort to avoid errors or omissions. Opinions, stories, and themes are intended for entertainment, motivation for research and future study. This book is nonfiction. The information provided within this book is for general informational and educational purposes only. The author makes no representations or warranties, express or implied, about the completeness, accuracy, reliability, suitability or availability with respect to the information, products, services, or related graphics contained in this book for any purpose. Any use of this information is at your own risk.

All Scripture quotations are from the The Holy Bible, King James Version, Pradis Software Rel 02.04.03, Built with Conform Version 5.00.0051, Version 5.1.50
Copyright ©2002 The Zondervan Corporation All Rights Reserved.

All rights reserved. This Publication may not be reproduced in whole or in part, stored or transmitted by any means. Media may use small portions for reviews. Please request written permission from Publisher for any other reason.

Printed in the United States of America

Dedication

To my husband of forty-four years,
and my family members who helped
the dream come true, by the grace of God.
We are overcomers.

Preface IX

Acknowledgements XI

Defining the forest escape XII

Introduction XIII

Chapter 1
Taking Honest Inventory 1

Chapter 2
Breaking Free 13

Chapter 3
Lighten Your Burdens 19

Chapter 4
Level of Dependency 25

Chapter 5
The Land of the Free 31

Chapter 6
Determine Necessities 35

Chapter 7
Homestead in Nature 43

Chapter 8
Ask for and Accept God's Blessings 51

Chapter 9
Water in All Seasons 57

Chapter 10
The Home of the Brave 63

Chapter 11
Food to Eat and for the Soul 77

Chapter 12
Explore the Forest 93

Chapter 13
Discover the Calm 101

Chapter 14
Warmth on a Cold Night 107

Chapter 15
Hunting and Security 115

Chapter 16
Preserving 123

Chapter 17
Medical / Emergencies 129

Chapter 18
Love Thy Neighbour 135

Chapter 19
Chickens and Coop 139

Chapter 20
Communication 149

Chapter 21
Sources of Income 153

Chapter 22
Sanitation 159

Chapter 23
Barter and Alliances 163

Chapter 24
Sustainability 167

Chapter 25
Minimum Investment 173

Chapter 26
Routine 177

Chapter 27
Trust Jesus 183

Chapter 28
God Answers Prayer 187

Chapter 29
Future Hope 191

Preface

Do you ever wonder what life could be like if you follow God's leading? Explore the idea of a forest escape. At any age, you could be living in nature, free from excessive debt, eating healthy food, building a new life, and learning new things every day! A chosen path is a deliberate choice. It won't happen by accident. It is a step in faith. Have the faith of a child and discover what God leads you to do!

If you are you wondering if you could work toward a balanced routine, enjoy great quality of life, cut out almost all debt, get rid of your home mortgage, live with less money, live off the land, be a stay-at-home mom/dad, be truly free and grow your own food, our story will help you!

We prayed and God revealed a path to follow. We chose to say no more regarding the stress, corruption, stress, high taxes and fast-paced life in New York State. This relaxed, conversational-style book was written so you can benefit from our experience making hard choices, selling everything, leaving family behind, building a cabin in Kentucky, and starting to live off the land in a secluded forest, with no running water. In the following years, our sons moved to our area, as well. The grandchildren now benefit from the choices we have made and are currently making. The adventure continues.

The idea of learning practical life skills as adults, and teaching the family members to grow food, do chores, care for animals, repair equipment, build, and hunt is vital. These basics have not been taught for generations and now need to be learned, as well as practiced. We don't know what the future brings, but we want to be prepared to not only survive but thrive!

We chose this path we are following, and it was with God's blessing that we have such a wonderful story to share.

Acknowledgements

Thank you, God, for your grace and all your blessings.
Thank you, Jesus, for your love, and for saving us from our sins.
Thank you, Holy Spirit, for being our guiding companion.

Psalms 100:3-5
Know ye that the LORD he is God:
it is he that hath made us, and not we ourselves;
we are his people, and the sheep of his pasture.
4 Enter into his gates with thanksgiving,
and into his courts with praise:
be thankful unto him, and bless his name.
5 For the LORD is good; his mercy is everlasting;
and his truth endureth to all generations.

A **forest escape**
is having land, nature, freedom, peace, quiet, and time with God.
It may not be the deep forest, but it is land God gives you to live on.
What you do with it is up to you!

God lays out **a chosen path** for you.
It is a direction for you to follow.

Your prayers are answered and you have confirmation
that it is God's will for your life.

It won't happen by accident
means that it is a deliberate choice
to follow God's path for your life.

Let's explore what the journey could be like!

An increasing number of people, in the USA and internationally, want to break free from the corporate grind and have a little place in the countryside, but they can't seem to conquer their fears or know what steps to take first to accomplish that goal. Everyone desires a healthy work/life balance and good quality of life, but few have it. Most people have trouble saying "*no more*" when pressured, or they look for approval from others before pursuing any personal dream. Most people spend too much of their hard-earned money, are buried in debt, have no money in savings and feel trapped in a job that causes incredible stress. Sometimes a big picture overview, a breakdown of steps to take, and a little encouragement can help us make informed decisions for sudden or gradual change.

You are invited to share our journey, to discover the benefit of getting rid of debt, see the idea of homesteading, explore various forest escape options, and begin to trust God in every step forward. A chosen path is one God lays out for you and you decide to choose to follow it. It has to be a deliberate decision. This lifestyle choice won't happen by accident.

In this book you will be discovering our journey, exploring options for yourself, and sharing our adventure to our forest escape. In nature, we withdraw from society and become closer to our Heavenly Father.

The private road to our forest escape is winding like a snake and treacherous if it is an icy winter day, but it is asphalt up to the public cemetery. After that, the abandoned road is dirt and gravel, and there is no county maintenance. We are on our own, as it is our responsibility. There are various types of simple-to-complex hunting camps along the way. There are two other homes at the end of the road. Our private driveway has a gate and the road into our land is winding, with a steep descent and a deep drop-off on the right side. Multiple seriously humorous signs warn that it is private land, and no trespassing is allowed. In summer, it is like a jungle with lush foliage. The wild roses and blackberry bushes scrape any vehicle traversing the driveway. We stop for a turtle or deer crossing the driveway each day. Sometimes, we must stop and use the chainsaw to cut a fallen tree out of the way, to get home. If it has torrentially rained, there are deep trenches from water runoff, and it is best to straddle those. We have to grade the driveway often with the tractor, to reclaim the gravel, and there is a ditch along the right side dug out deeply, in an attempt to channel water and prevent erosion. The driveway ascent is steep and winding coming up out of the gully that floods from time to time, despite the drainage pipe under the road. With an extra burst of speed, we arrive at the top wide-open clearing where the 2-story cabin is located. If it is dusk, the glow of warm light can be seen in all windows of this cozy cabin. Many family members helped build this home. This is the home that love built. If it is a sunny fall afternoon, the oranges and golds of the trees are breathtaking! Many mornings, a peaceful gentle fog is amongst the trees. Looking around you see a storage building, lean-to, generator, stacked wood on pallets, security system cameras, various equipment, and vehicles. If you walk around the cabin, there is a greenhouse, huge garden, chicken coop and compost bin. The land is rich with oak and cedar trees, various species of birds, deer, turkeys, coyotes, and rabbits. Logging roads throughout the 43 acres of property allow access with ATVs and UTVs. Welcome to our forest escape!

We could live off the land and never leave if we wanted to. In a crisis, we don't need to go to the city. We have supplies and sustainable solutions. We are happy homesteading and living in solitude. This is God's country. This is our sanctuary.

One step at a time, discover how we followed the path that God set before us. We had to make a conscious decision to break free from a stressful life. We had to agree to sell everything, leave family members behind, and start over in a new place with a few basic items, and a dream. There was a forest, a very long muddy driveway and nothing more. Everything had to be planned and built. There was no water well or municipal water. It felt like being a pioneer, and it is a wonderful continuing adventure. You will see how things start out, change, and develop over time, as we learn and experience different aspects of living in a forest escape. All the while, you can think about the various aspects and how they might pertain to your life.

If you want wholesome and nutritious food, you can have it! You can be proud of the food that you grow yourself and you can have that beautiful garden you have always wanted. You can preserve food for the winter months. You can raise chickens and have fresh eggs every morning. You can go hunting and bring back dinner and fill your freezer for the year. You can forage in the forest for wild onions, berries, and mushrooms. All the while, you are learning new things.

Broken. If you look around, you may personally observe one or more of these changes in life. Maybe not. I am just putting it out there to think about. Considering what is broken is the first step in trying to find a solution.

As an overview, the big picture of life in general seems not only stressful and unhealthy, but economically unsustainable. Under constant bombardment of advertising to buy more, and the emphasis of materialism, the average person is buried in debt with high interest rates, under stress, and suffers from depression or anxiety. Influencers portray perfection and desire that is virtually impossible to achieve, and unfulfilling if attained. Individuality, tools for handling adversity, and compassion are dying.

The communistic hive mentality of one government queen and all the rest citizen worker bees, believes that we should tolerate everything, own nothing, and become desensitized concerning the loss of freedom and lack of emotions or human touch. It is an ever-growing phenomenon. Privacy is offered up in the name of convenience. Freedom is sacrificed in the name of false security. Lack of constitutional pushback by citizens has been allowing the government of the republic to go from servant to master.

We are changing from thinking for ourselves, to wanting to be told what to do. This is not the America of our forefathers, and we are being discouraged from being those strong individuals who not only dream but fulfill those dreams. The unique ideas are disparaged: we should all be alike, compliant and of one opinion. It happens gradually, so people are not aware of how far we have gone down this slippery slope, losing our freedom. Or we can consider the idea that we are allowing our freedom to be taken away. Evil prevails when good men do nothing.

All media seems to control the narrative and is telling a story that is not recognizable in everyday life. The virtual reality media channels are telling us stories of what is happening in life. We look around and do not see any of it. A lot of it simply isn't true – it is an agenda. It is fake life. It causes fear.

Our freedom is under attack. Corruption, high taxes, and inflation make it impossible to live a middle-class life. Land and property ownership is punished by exorbitant taxes, so that people could lose their homes, farms, vehicles, equipment, and livelihood. If citizens own nothing and pay rent, they will do that until they die. If citizens accumulate wealth and pay off their mortgages, they will have no payments when they retire, and they can leave homes and businesses to their children when they die. The wealth is passed on from one generation to the next.

Evil is saturating many aspects of our society, is gaining a stronghold, and seeks to destroy Christian values, the church, the family unit, and the children. With so much noise, pollution and crime in cities, the distractions keep people running to and fro, too busy to enjoy life, be thankful, or listen to God. It is an unsatisfying routine of chaos. People try to fit God into their lives once a week if they can find a church that hasn't forgotten its first love: Jesus. Parents find little or no time with their children because earning a living is so demanding and paying the bills is almost impossible.

Health is an issue. Food has low nutritional value, is filled with additives, fillers, hormones, pesticides, herbicides, and more. Work/life balance is out of proportion.

Not to feel an overload of negativity and not that you might have experienced all of these things, but probably at least one of these topics hits home for you.

Fixed. Pray and ask God for direction in your life. Explore alternatives that would be wholesome in terms of lifestyle. Separate from evil. Read the Bible and study God's Word. Follow God's leading, look for confirmation, and choose a new path. It doesn't happen by accident. It requires a deliberate decision. Take control of your life. Be a good manager of time and a good steward of resources. Rely on God and develop faith by taking the first step. This book will show you our path taken to a forest escape, what we have discovered, our quality of life that we have achieved, and our preparations for the future.

As an entrepreneur, I have always embraced risk and followed my dreams, and as a woman married for 44 years, we have encountered many trials, but experienced many more moments of joy. I am currently semi-retired. My husband served in the military, was self-employed, and was employed in management, but is retired now.

Blessed by God with spiritual gifts, natural talents, and learned skills, I have a heart for God's work, and don't hesitate when God motivates me to complete a project. I am a teacher, an author, an artist, a producer of custom gifts, a web developer, a builder, and a homesteader. Using online platforms, and my web site Forest Escape Christian Gifts dot com, I sell custom Christian gifts.

As the owner of MediaTek Grafx, a full-service advertising agency started in 2001, I was a workaholic for over 30 years, functioning with only four hours of sleep per night. Before finally breaking free from the corporate grind, I worked with various businesses, churches, utilities, counterterrorism efforts, schools, and organizations.

In the past, I also voluntarily produced a monthly prayer letter for missionaries in Africa for many years. I spent hours on social media (before censorship was an issue) writing to, and praying for, pastors and good Samaritans running orphanages all around the world. It was emotionally exhausting and I really admire those who are prayer warriors.

As a web developer and writer, I maintain my first labor of love, the Christian web site, Faithful Watchmen dot com.

In 2014, I began writing and publishing Christian books, for children and adults, through MediaTek Grafx. I co-authored a book with my best friend. I am the author of six Christian children's books to date. I also wrote, designed and published a prayer journal.

Working as a teacher in various capacities, I worked with a youth group and a technical institute to promote self-employment and business ethics, and I am currently teaching communication skills internationally. I also taught mosaic workshops, and I taught a Christian creative writing class at a Christian assisted living facility, to help the elderly patients write books to give to their loved ones.

Communication is a passion for me. This book is a conversational style that is very relaxed and a quick read. I encourage you to enjoy the adventure.

Now more than ever, it is important to break free if you are thinking about a lifestyle change, such as a forest escape. The prices of land are increasing at an alarming rate, we have shortages of building products, and inflation to think about. Debt is increasing and interest rates are unbearable. It is hard to continue living in the urban or suburban manner everyone seems to enjoy: the modern lifestyle is almost impossible to maintain, financially. Social decline is steady, evil is getting a stronghold, and a place of rest or reflection is important. You can choose to withdraw from society in a rural area and become closer to God. Personally, we should have started this journey years ago, when a little younger, but we are very thankful for our forest escape we have today.

It is hoped that you will be inspired by our story to commit to change, to set goals for your future, and to become closer to God the Father; Jesus, the Son, and the Holy Spirit who lives within you. Some ideas work for some people - and not all ideas work for all people. Whatever you read in this book is about one type of adventure. It is our adventure. Your adventure will be different in many ways. It can become a journey of self-discovery and what could work for you. Points will be made, some successes and failures will be shared, as well as ideas will be presented that worked for our lifestyle journey. The disclaimer is that this book showcases what we did, and I, as the author, am not liable for how it works out for you! If you are wanting to feel hope, to appreciate daily blessings, and to thank God for life itself, read this book with anticipation. Forest Escape a chosen path is our story, it will help you step out in faith, and it is an honor to share it with you!

Chapter 1 – Taking Honest Inventory

Psalms 26:2 Examine me, O Lord, and prove me; try my reins and my heart.

Take a deep breath. It is time to be honest – brutally honest. You have already decided a lifestyle change is worth exploring. That is a good step. The next step is to look at how unmanageable life has become, compared to how you really want life to be. When you see the stark difference between what you want and what you have now, you will be motivated to put forth the effort needed to literally choose a new path.

are your priorities, in order?
Are you wanting more time, lots of money, parties with friends, time with family, to put God first, serve your country, corporate promotions, business success or something else?

Write a sentence that truly objectively describes what is going on in your life right now. Write what has prioritized your time, and write how fulfilled and happy you are. If you write a sentence describing the ideal top three priorities, what do you want them to be? Write them down in order of priority. Though you are not sure how, this is what you will be working toward. Don't worry about the "how" because God has that all figured out for you. It will be up to you to pray and listen to His will for your life. You really can live the ideal life that God has planned for you.

For me, as a Christian, God should be number one in terms of priorities, then family two and country three. As you notice, when considering the top three, work isn't even on my short list. You say, well you have to make money to eat. I would argue that God won't let you starve. Put Him first and all other things will fall in place. Also, this short list is about love, duty and commitment. Isn't the heart what matters most? Any time we put something else as number one, isn't it like worshipping that thing? Isn't that like an idol? God hates idols. So, if

God is first, we have no worries after that. In all things, ask God in prayer. Any time God is not first, He lets us make mistakes that teach us a lesson. We can't put God first only when we have hard times. So, getting our lives in order means worshipping God and putting Him first each day.

 ### do you define success?
What really makes you excited about life? Do you want prestige, money, good family, to be good at sports, good housekeeping, to be a good parent, or some other goal?

God's perspective on success is probably how much you love Him, use the gifts He gave you, and how often you obey Him. Jesus said to love God, to love ourselves, and to love our neighbors. That wasn't just good advice – it was a commandment. Think about what you want to focus on, versus what you are actually focusing on at the moment. As you see, we are rethinking everything. It is about breaking free and doing what we really believe. Don't worry about the steps to get there. Simply mentally commit to what you feel is right, learn what God wants you to do with your life and see where He wants you to live. It takes a step in faith.

 ### are your natural skills?
Most people have God-given talents, things they can easily do, and do better than other people.

We also have skills that we were naturally born with and they will help us accomplish great things. Some people grow plants, some repair everything that breaks or breaks down, and some people build things. What are you really good at? It is not helpful to say that you have no skills. Maybe you have not practiced them recently, but there are things you are good at. Maybe it is something you are not great at, but you love to do it. Follow your heart and use that natural talent. Share that natural talent with kids and grandkids.

 ### are your gifts from God?
These are spiritual gifts. God gives each person gifts. We were born with special gifts from God. Learn about the gifts and see what yours are. The gifts are from God and include wisdom, knowledge, faith, healing, miracles, discernment, tongues, prophecy, mercy, administration, exhortation, apostles, evangelists, interpretation of tongues, pastors, and teachers.

You will want to work for God's purpose in your life. Consider these when you think about the future. As saved Christians, we cannot stop working after being saved. There is much work to do in this world, and we are called to use our gifts. We are called to share the Gospel of Jesus with everyone. What if the rapture happens and someone you love is left behind? Be motivated by that and get busy!

are your learned skills?
Maybe you have been educated in construction, plumbing, farming, preserving food, finance, etc. The real question is do you like doing those things, in the environment you now operate in?

Just because you were educated in something, doesn't mean you actually want to continue doing that job. How can you apply what you know to homesteading and simplifying? Most learned skills can be applied to any situation. The other idea is that you will need to study and learn many new things for your forest escape. The skills you need will be developed over time, with each new experience.

you able to set boundaries?
Are you good at saying no, managing stress, and knowing the difference between acceptable and unacceptable?

When anything becomes overwhelming, you need to be able to feel that increasing stress, and have a plan. Watch for the way you tend to handle things. Are you reactive or proactive? You can practice, even now, to see if you have what it takes to handle a lifestyle change that is critical. Is your schedule always planned by others, or do you block time off in each day or week that allows you to do your job properly? Are you able to say the word "no" when so many people make demands of your time? Many times, if people are under stress, it is because they are allowing it. Everyone is a manager.

They are either good at controlling their workflow and work environment, or they are constantly under stress. We are not good managers if we are suffering. The expression take the bull by the horns is relevant and important. Over time, with experience, we develop the ability to handle more, in an intelligent way.

 **you have the ability to manage multiple projects?** Think about the big picture, individual projects, and phases within each timeline.

The big picture in homesteading is what you ideally want to accomplish someday. But reality is prioritizing what you need immediately, so you can take baby steps in each project to get started. As time goes on, you can enter the next phase and accomplish more. Some things are controlled by seasons, health, rain, mood, money, and more internal or external factors. Always in the back of your mind, you plan for corrections, changes, and expansion. This is a fluid process. Think agile.

It is important to have a one year plan. Each month has objectives and of course it is good to plan around the seasons and weather. The monthly projects/tasks are broken into the four weeks. Working a little on multiple projects should be something you enjoy and are willing to handle.

 **a balanced life is attainable**
Divide 24 hours into work, sleep and family/sports/hobbies and see how that can work for you. Practice, even now, seeing how strong you are and how committed you are.

Try balancing your current life into three parts. Work gets eight hours plus one hour of commuting round trip plus or minus a little, sleep gets eight hours, and the family/exercise/hobbies category gets seven hours. If you can balance these items, you will be happier and healthier. So many people are on antianxiety and antidepressant medicines, which have bad side effects. A large percentage of the USA workforce is on these meds. We must respect ourselves and demand respect from others. We cannot say yes until it hurts. Marriages and children suffer. Our mental and physical health suffers when our life is out of balance. We can't sacrifice our health, spouses and children, just to make the boss happy. Again, priorities matter the most.

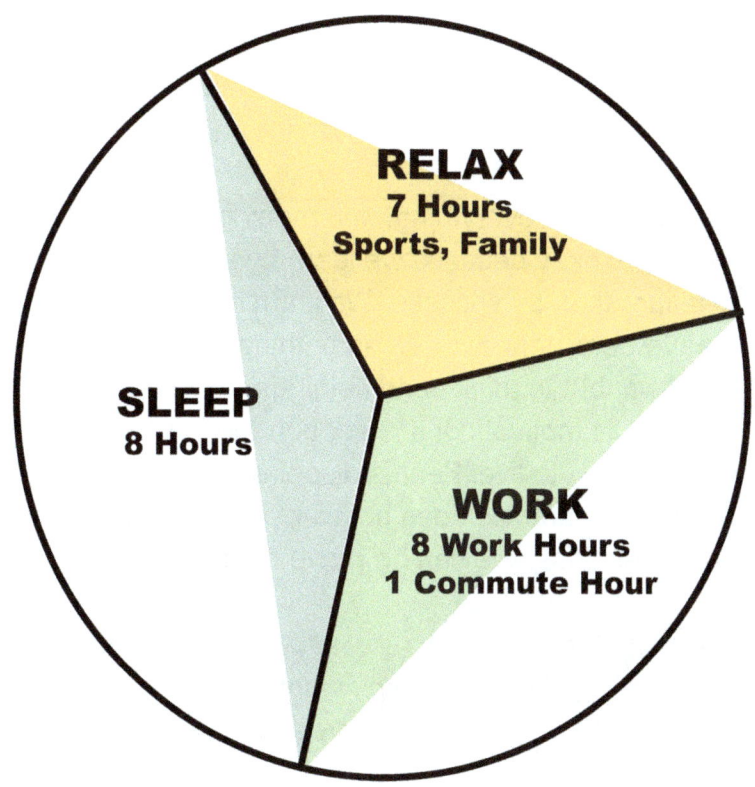

 **can discover your dreams**
What you have always wanted is what you can work toward. Maybe it will take time, but the idea is that you work toward it and that gives you hope. Most of the time what drives us, and really is a passion of the heart, is something we can use to bless others and serve God.

Dreams are special and should never be ignored. What makes you think that you can't attain your dreams? Growing up, I wanted to do so many things! I knew that if I dreamed it, I could do it! It could be one dream or many. With God's blessing the most amazing things can happen! What you feel is impossible, God makes possible. Don't allow anyone to take away that enthusiasm for life. Writing this book, people may not find it appealing or well-written or criticize it in some way, but that will not stop me from writing the book. If God uses it to help only one other person, I will feel that the effort was worth every minute. I simply put it out there and let God use it, whatever it may be, for His purpose. Nothing is for me. I share what I am led to share because God has impressed it upon my heart. Each of us should dream big - and follow our dreams!

are your fears?

Many people are worried about failing, life being too demanding, not having enough knowledge, not having enough money to do everything, not having enough food to eat, or not knowing how to start on a new path.

Nobody knows everything, and many of us know just enough to get into a lot of trouble. But, that's okay because we learn by trial and error. It is okay to fail. We learn more by failure than by success. We learn about ourselves – what we are capable of – and to have persistence to see something through to completion. It is natural to fear the unknown, but to think of something really great happening - to change the quality of life you live - is motivating! It is enough fuel for the fire to get the job done. We can't say that we are afraid to live. Fear is dispelled by experience and by trusting God. God gives us the strength and He does not want us to be timid. He really doesn't like timid behavior as it is faithless. We can be brave because He guides us and gives us strength.

do you really feel free?

Do you want to be free to grow your own food, free to enjoy nature, free to hunt, and free to worship?

Are you able to choose how much time you spend with family, around your home and with nature? Most people, all around the world, wish for more time and more money. It is a trade-off: you can have time and not much money, or you can have money but not much time. If you eliminate debt and cut expenses, then money is not a predominant factor anymore. You can enjoy your family and nature, in a forest escape! You can also be safe from chaos, persecution, inflation, and crime. God made us a free people. Freedom is not free: it is a battle to preserve.

Soldiers fight to preserve our freedom. It is sad, but many average citizens today would give it all away: they would trade freedom for socialism or communism. People think convenience is best, and that the government will protect them. This republic in the USA is meant to have small government serving the people. We are not slaves to the government, and yet the more we depend on the social programs of the government, the less freedom we have. We, in effect, set the government up as the master, because we get social program free stuff. That problem of embracing socialism is because people take freedom for granted and have never lost it. They don't understand or know history, so they are doomed to repeat it.

With advanced technology people trade privacy and security for convenience every day. They are fine with IoT Internet of Things total connections that can be hacked and Cloud-based data centers that do not even have background checks for employees, and social media platforms that are known to be Chinese or Qatar spy programs. Social media censorship is being tolerated, eliminating freedom or speech. Citizens do not question anything, nor guard against these hazards – they actually know the dangers and costs - but they desire these apps and conveniences anyway.

 **much debt do you have?**
Are you heavily encumbered with debt and a slave to your job, spending too much, or saving like crazy?

Let's think about debt. People give advice and say to save money, but then you can never enjoy life and do fun things now. All work and no play is no way to live. So really, it isn't about saving money – it is about not acquiring excessive debt. A tiny house, building with cash or selling an expensive home to buy a small home with proceeds are all ways to have no mortgage. Ignoring society's push to make you buy the newest and best fad is really important. We have to choose not to succumb to this pressure. No debt is like having a ton of savings. Money in savings could devalue and be wiped out in an economic crisis. You could leave the work environment and not worry for quite some time. Society pushes us to think one way, and we get on the hamster wheel and run and run. If we think for ourselves, we will definitely have a better quality of life. When we separate from the world and commit to living the life God plans for us, we are set free.

Commit to the idea of not having debt, using cash only to pay for things, and start planning for your forest escape. In a year, you could be buying the land and building a small cabin. We have to get the monkey off our back. Debt is overwhelming and not healthy. So many people have a mortgage of $200,000 or $700,000, two cars that are $60,000 or more, and credit card debt that is something they can never pay off without a serious change of mind and immediate action. How did they get into this situation? How did you get into this type of situation? We are all pretty much the same. We fell for the hype, the commercialism, the idea that easier is better, and that we need what we buy. Of course, most things could have been repaired not replaced, the house could have been smaller or less expensive and in a different neighborhood, and the used cars we had were just fine. The credit cards did not need to be used, but the fads and the hype convinced us to buy something we didn't have enough money for. It was a trap and we were ensnared. We literally are a slave to our debt. We are a slave to material things. Be brave and sell the expensive stuff, buy used and buy less. Be free. Again, we have to make up our minds that we are doing this. If we never make it to the forest escape, at least go this far. Be free wherever you are.

 **you have what it takes?**
Are you motivated and energetic, and able to fight for the things in life that matter most to you?

You already know what it is like to fight in the corporate world, in society and in the streets. You haven't quit when it all was difficult. Yet. You might make a choice to leave the circus, but it won't be quitting. It will be a conscious choice and a chosen path. God lights the way, answers prayers, sends confirmation and blesses you, if it is His will for you to change your lifestyle.

A forest escape is having land, nature, freedom, peace, and time with God. It may not be the deep forest, but it is land God gives you to live on. What you do with it is up to you!

The idea of blood, sweat and tears in this forest escape lifestyle choice is real. You will probably get hurt, get slivers, twist your ankle, cut your hand, fall down, and bleed. The sweat of hard work is never ending, but you can embrace the morning sunrise or early evening hours and work in cooler weather. You can work smarter instead of working harder, sometimes. The tears come when the work is almost overwhelming, a bunny passes away, or a chicken dies, or the day's 6-hour project was a failure.

Some people feel alone and they can feel lonely, too. As Christians, we have to remember that we are never alone. Jesus made sure of that. We have the Holy Spirit who is not only with us - but inside us. We are never alone! Tears can also be from joy and thankfulness to God. Some days, in the gently laid morning fog, I see a doe and a fawn walking slowly across my yard and down into the forest. At this point, all perseverance to get to this point in life has been worth it. The idea is that you fight and never quit. Know in advance that it isn't easy to make a lifestyle change. What you are doing now isn't easy either, but you continue marching on. The forest escape is a constant effort to persevere, as well.

Keep in mind that there are many homesteaders, survivalists, preppers, and others, in a network all around the world to help you when you get stuck. Buy the books, watch the online videos, study the web sites and print articles, and more! Don't count on electricity and the internet for your knowledge. Have a library of information for all pertinent subjects. Save the articles in binders, to have as a handy reference.

taking Inventory is Done

So, some things are doable, and some things seem difficult. That is how we felt, too. But having the fight and zest for life is motivational and God's blessing will carry you on.

We are all children in God's eyes. Our Heavenly Father helps us each step of the way if we let Him. You took mental inventory, so now let's continue on with practical aspects of following your chosen path to a forest escape. If you decide to pursue a lifestyle change, you get the idea of what you are getting into. At this point there is no actual risk in this mental exercise. You are just imagining the adventure, so enjoy it.

Matthew 7:14 Because strait is the gate, and narrow is the way, which leadeth unto life, and few there be that find it.

Chapter 2 – Breaking Free

2 Corinthians 6:17 Wherefore come out from among them, and be ye separate, saith the Lord,

If you have had enough of the saturation of society, the pressures of social media, the exceedingly presumptuous behavior of bosses, the daily schedule beyond your control, and the excessive debt and stress, you can walk away from all of the aspects that are not healthy. If you need medicines to handle stress or anxiety, maybe life is not healthy.

Matthew 22:37-39 Jesus said unto him, Thou shalt love the Lord thy God with all thy heart, and with all thy soul, and with all thy mind. This is the first and great commandment. And the second is like unto it, Thou shalt love thy neighbour as thyself.

Regular life without God is not enough. So many people strive for something that isn't attainable or something that is attainable and they get what they want, but are not happy. We grieve for people who commit suicide. Even Christians just quit life. Some people don't physically die, but they are spiritually dead. The time is now, to wake up and see with eyes that see, and hear with ears that hear! If you see someone struggling, help them. We are commanded to love our neighbors. Jesus commanded it. Agape love is a love that sees no petty differences - it is something so much more. It is unconditional love. People are struggling because they are working toward the wrong things. If everyone looks to God first, then they will have a special kind of love that helps them through anything. Life has trials, but with God we can be happy.

Our soldiers, veterans, their families all have such pressures living two lives. One life is of sacrifice, trauma, injury and PTSD, and then coming back to the "normal" life and "normal society" to see people who are not cherishing their freedom: the citizens seem happy to give it all away. That in itself is heartbreaking. Many military jobs don't translate to average citizen jobs after military service is over.

You don't have to feel pressure living in this society if you are military. Withdraw into your own land and have your own peace, with God. It is preferable to be alone with our Father in Heaven, as opposed to being together with people in society. God loves you and wants you to live the best life possible, doing His work. Over time He reveals what He wishes for you to do.

Be patient and soldier on. Seriously, one battle at a time and the war will be won. There is a war of evil against good. Soon, the antichrist will be revealed. Then, we will see that we are all soldiers. The antichrist will be against Jesus Christ. Of course, we know God wins, but we must help those who are not saved. We will be persecuted. Active and prior military can help those with no training when we are all persecuted for being Christians. There are many jobs to do. A special thank you goes out to all who served, are serving or will serve soon. We are fighting a spiritual battle, so prepare.

> **Get started today, don't procrastinate. Once you have pondered all these points in chapter one, write down your answers in complete sentences. Read them out loud. Believe it or not, at that point, you have established a possible plan for your life. That is normally the most difficult for many people!**

Many people say that they want to write a book. It is quite easy to grab a piece of paper and start to write, or to start a new word processor document and save it to your hard drive. At that point you are an author. You have started to write a book. The dread of starting is over. The fear is gone. You have put a dream into motion. So many people won't write their book because they could not do that one simple task. It literally takes two minutes to make that spark into a fire! But fear floods in like a torrential rainstorm and drowns that dream. Be brave and persistent. Start and never stop. It is exciting to personally live life to the utmost, instead of watching others fulfill their dreams. Don't let opportunity pass you by.

You are free to choose. So many people feel that they are slaves to a system, society, their boss or their company. Our lifestyle was handed down from one generation to another. People felt stuck and could not change. Every day is a new day and filled with choices. Think about what freedom really means. Think it and live it. You are about to become a rebel! You can question everything you have been told, coerced into and have been living all your life. This lifestyle choice is a mindset. You have to really want a change and be willing to work really hard for it. Freedom is never free, and it is a continual battle to live free. You have heard the expression blood, sweat and tears; this is truly applicable for a life of freedom.

> **A decision to explore can be at any age. If you are young and just starting out, it is the perfect time to consider a forest escape. If you are retirement age, it is the perfect way to settle down.**

Do we choose good or bad? Lots of people feel they have to live in the gray area – not really good and not really all bad. This causes a lot of people to make choices that hurt them later in life. Stick with good choices, for good reasons. There are no bad choices for good reasons. That gets you into trouble. Are you able to think for yourself? Do you follow the crowd? Do you depend on the admiration and validation of social media, to feel like a complete and acceptable person? The difference between right and wrong is not how many people agree with you. The difference between right and wrong is determined by God and written in the Word of God. Choose good and ask for God's blessing. Read the Bible; let the Holy Spirit speak.

When we think about evil and its influence in this world, it is complex. It has a name and it is Satan. It is real and always trying to kill, steal and destroy. The strategies are many. Satan casts doubt, distracts you, deceives you and causes destruction of your life and damnation is the result if you are not a born-again Christian. Jesus teaches us to have reliance on God, allows us to have resolution and gives us many revelations over the period of our lifetime. We need a revival internally to bravely live more for God each day, because we know in the end we are redeemed and going to heaven. Don't forget Satan exists but don't give evil too much time in your day: concentrate on God. Choose, each day, what Jesus would do or advise us to do in all things.

Satan	or	Jesus
Doubt	or	Reliance
Distraction	or	Resolution
Deception	or	Revelation
Destruction	or	Revival
Damnation	or	Redemption

Breaking free means a separation and a relief from something that is too much. It is a new path forward. It can be a routine, a concept, or a mindset, as well as a physical condition that we want to break free from. Thinking for yourself is important. Don't consider anyone else's input in making decisions. Pray and ask God what to do. Change your routines and start each day studying God's Word and having prayer time. Enjoy time in nature, which God created, and come back to peace of mind. We stray so far from that calm in daily life and we hardly take a moment to enjoy anything. That stress is really unacceptable. First we have to embrace the idea of changing our minds. Then our actions follow. If we have extreme faith we act first trusting God, and then our minds follow. Whichever category you are in, let the adventure begin!

I was a workaholic for many years, but I did prioritize and put family concerns first. I was always a chaperone on school field trips with the kids and their friends. If the kids were sick, I didn't work. I was self-employed most of the years that the children were young. I could control my time and my priorities. I worked from 6 AM until 2 AM each day, and then slept four hours per night. Looking back now, I know that is no way to live. I was driven by the idea that having enough money to provide extra things was really a benefit. In fact, that isn't true. It was predominantly a waste of time. We each have to learn for ourselves and make our own mistakes. I gave more time to clients than family. As a wife and mom, I now know it should be the other way around.

Growing up in a good family, without money and less stuff, is the best teacher. Children appreciate everything and take nothing for granted. Luckily, we had times with money and times without money, so everyone learned to appreciate most things. We also learned that we had so much fun as family, that money didn't matter as long as we could eat just fine.

Being a part of the lives of our children is vital. Any family that is suffering has parents who are not paying attention to the children, are spoiling the children out of guilt for not being home, or they have a single-parent family. Parents have the difficult role, and are not the friends of their children, so they have to have tough love. The family unit is so important, for love, nurturing, growing and handling struggles. Today, most children and young adults cannot handle adversity. They don't have the tools to work with. They never discovered how to handle the many things that go wrong in life. We have generations of young people that were provided material things, but not the life lessons they needed, nor the love they so desperately wanted. The children and young people need hope, just like the older adults. God gives us hope.

Every week can include fun activities, and not just on the holidays.

Resolve to do the right things, as soon as you can. Don't delay. Break free from the vicious circle that keeps people on a hamster wheel going nowhere. What does breaking free literally mean to you?

We always wanted 30 acres of land and to build from scratch. God blessed us with 43 acres and we gave 13 acres to our oldest son and his wife, for helping us build our cabin. God blesses us with more than we ask for, for reasons we do not yet know. We did not know at that time, what the future would bring.

Chapter 3 – Lighten Your Burdens

Matthew 11:28-30 Come unto me, all ye that labour and are heavy laden, and I will give you rest. Take my yoke upon you, and learn of me; for I am meek and lowly in heart: and ye shall find rest unto your souls. For my yoke is easy, and my burden is light.

Selling possessions, downsizing, and getting rid of debt will get rid of many burdens. Leave financial encumbrance and stress behind; find peace.

> Keeping the used vehicle, selling the expensive home and using proceeds to build a cabin, paying off credit cards, etc., will help you feel less stress. Selling possessions and not buying new items when you can repair existing items will help you break free from debt.

If and when you decide to sell your home, you can take the profits to build your new living quarters. That means in the future you will have no home mortgage. Retirement, financial crisis or losing your job could be devastating if you have a mortgage.

Credit cards can be a downfall. Our mistake was keeping them after they had a zero balance, so cut those rascals into 30 pieces with scissors. Then burn them. Then celebrate, as those credit cards are the biggest ball and chain you will ever encounter. Their temptation whispers to you every time you are in a store, use your phone or use computer browser. Get rid of all cards, except one for emergencies. Remember, it is said that you don't own possessions – they own you!

Do you want to stop working for others, retire or work part-time? In business we think about diversification or deriving income from many sources. We cannot have all our eggs in one basket. Lighten your stress by generating some extra cash from different revenue streams.

There is a choice to stop buying things. It is a choice to limit the cost you pay for gifts for birthdays and Christmas. It is a choice to make gifts, from the heart, that become sentimental possessions. Commercialism is great for making a living, but we don't want to become entrapped in a system that promotes consumerism only. We must be producers. It isn't just a corporate perspective, it is personal, too. Consider making gifts for family members. Teach new skills, so they can also make gifts.

It is important to think about the future and leaving the world of financial stress. Are investments safe? Is currency turning into digital? It is. Should we have precious metals? Maybe. When it is all said and done, none of that would matter in a crisis. The fundamental currency would be the bartering of water, ammunition, seeds, and food. If things go wrong in the future, nothing would be worth more than clean water, healthy food, and good tools. This is also good for planning retirement as you may not have savings, but you won't have debt either. Also, you will have a way of life that provides food, possibly free heat and a low cost of living. That brings peace of mind.

> **If you desire independence, you can pay off debts, sell the home, cash out what you can and plan the new start. A simple life means everything is smaller, less stressful, and less expensive in the long run. Look up the concepts: minimalism, tiny house living, off-the-grid living, secluded living, and no-mortgage homes. You can make a choice as to what will be a good start for you. Remember, in the future small things may change as time goes by.**

Minimalism

Minimalism is getting rid of stuff, so when you do that you are generating some cash by selling off things you don't need. Think 1800s living and save the buckets, baskets, shovels, cookware and blankets. Sell the decorative things with no purpose and all the clothes with limited functionality and practicality. Sell 50 junk items for $1 at a garage sale and buy some good used tools. The idea of minimalism is that you own your stuff and your stuff doesn't own you. That means no more credit card charges for fads, fashion trends and every new gadget that comes along. Sell the designer clothes and buy good work jeans, a heavy jacket and some leather gloves. Sell the expensive handbag and buy a canvas wood sling for carrying firewood or a nice wheelbarrow for gardening. If you look around your home and check out what you own, which items would serve you well if the power went out or you had to survive like a pioneer? Most of the items that people own have no purpose when it comes down to survival life.

Tiny house living

Tiny house living is pretty interesting, as this type of home is towed by your own truck or delivered and put in place by a transport company. Your tiny home could be moved seasonally, to be near family, or where you find work. The cost of the home is a one-time up front cost, without a long-lasting mortgage hanging over your head. The budget could be $20,000 to $100,000. The square footage has to be thought through completely. It could be possible that a person would go crazy in too small of a space, if the outdoor area was not also living space during one particular season or another. Usually this type of home has deck space for outdoor cooking and seating. A reasonable size for a tiny home could be 400 or 500 square feet for two to four people. The home could be 8-1/2 feet wide by 13-1/2 feet high by 40 feet long, or as law dictates or towing allows. The second floor would be a sleeping loft or storage most likely. The ceilings are low, usually 6-1/2 feet, so you want lots of windows. This would be fine, as homesteading life is spent more outdoors than in doors.

Off-the-grid living

Off-the-grid living means that you will not have all of the municipal utilities. Some people live completely off-gird and other people have some services. Living without water means you need a creek, artesian well or drilled water well. Rain collection is probably not going to be enough for garden, drinking and animals. You may need a cistern and haul water. Living without a toilet to a sewer system means having a composting toilet or an outhouse. Living without electricity means using a generator, solar or wind for power generation. Otherwise, you live using candles, lanterns and hurricane lamps for light. Anything you might have used electricity for would be eliminated, unless you run a generator once a day. Living without garbage collection means that you have less waste by design and compost as much as possible. Repurpose and reuse containers and packaging. Living without internet and phone service means using a CB radio or HAM radio for news and communication, or driving somewhere to connect if you have a device, or simply speaking to local people for the news of the day.

Secluded living

Secluded living is what our forest escape is considered. The idea is to have enough land to be separate from other people, and to have privacy to live freely. We have roads on our property. A gate can be locked on the private road and on the driveway. We only have one neighbor, other than family, at a fair distance and a few hunting camps along the private road. When we live our everyday life, we do not need to see other people for any reason. We can be completely separate in our secluded location. Our intention is to live off the land and to be off-grid in the future, if need be. Nobody cares if the dog barks, the hens cluck and the roosters crow.

No-mortgage homes

No-mortgage homes are homes that you can build, according to your budget, with cash and no bank assistance/indebtedness. Getting a structure in place that protects you from the elements is the first step. The rest is internal and can progress as money allows. Of course, you need a kitchen area and functional bathroom. I think the biggest part of this journey is to slow down and be patient in your thinking about accomplishing projects. I have had to take it a little slower and really just be thankful for what I have, and what we have accomplished. We, in the USA, have the mentality to want it all - and to have it all right now. This new way of thinking is to have what you need to get by, and later you will have more. It is doubtful that we will have it all so to speak. There is something more desired most of the time, but it isn't really a necessary item. The old expressions our grandparents would say: good enough for now, someday and just get by. Freedom from a huge mortgage is so wonderful that I have a hard time describing that. If you want to say you own something, you can't be indebted to the bank. We are proud to say our home is not perfect, but it is perfect for us and it is ours.

> In our story, we have so much more than we imagined, through God's blessing. It would have been fine to have a tiny one-room cabin with an outhouse. That is how badly we wanted to break free from the NY State society we previously lived in, the exorbitant taxes we paid, the stress, the organized corruption all around us, the lack of freedom, and the debt.

Your home

Whatever home idea you have, plan a budget that you feel will work. Then, have 25% more as a safety net, if you can. Everything costs more than you imagine and with a volatile economy and supply shortages (meaning higher prices), it gets out of control quickly. If you are tough, getting by is enough. You can start this journey without a big safety net, as we did. However, if you tend to get stressed out easily, have the money set aside to get the things you feel are vital when you need them. It is a transitional period and, unfortunately, you may have to rely on charge cards for some critical items.

It is a test of patience. We started out with $30,000 in cash. It turned out to be enough to have a great start on our 24 ft. x 32 ft. 2-story cabin, but we lived seven years without tongue and groove wood on the walls, so we looked at studs and insulation during that whole time. We had to wait until we had $5,000 for the wall wood. If you can be patient and live with that kind of thing, then you will probably be fine!

Changing lifestyle choices means that you are in control of keeping your family safe in the event of any type of chaos or upheaval. If you depend on money to help you survive, or the government, those two resources won't help you in a crisis. The place you choose to live and the way you live, will help you. It would not be great to live in a city if there were riots and chaos, compared to the secluded forest escape with the garden you grow and chickens you raise for food.

Lighten your burdens, get educated, learn new stuff, and reduce your stress.

It is a step in faith. Pray about your path forward. See where God leads you. Meanwhile, let's continue pursuing this mental journey and see how it could work out!

Chapter 4 – Level of Dependency

1 Timothy 6:17 Charge them that are rich in this world, that they be not highminded, nor trust in uncertain riches, but in the living God, who giveth us richly all things to enjoy;

How independent will you be? Where is the future going? Will inflation cause utilities to be unsustainable? Do you want to pay for utilities or live off-grid now or in the future? Will you continue working at your job, or will you create an income source from your land? Maybe you could derive income from logging on your land and selling firewood.

If you want complete independence, it means no more utilities and you have to provide for all of your needs. Imagine long-term camping. If you want to gradually work to that level, it will need to be planned in small steps over time. Think about where you will be comfortable and how that might change if you disconnect even more. Maybe your plan or layout for your homestead will be different. Just keep that in the back of your mind. The beauty of this discovery is that everything changes as we mature and feel comfortable trying new things!

> We have utilities, but we know that one day we may not. We have a plan for water and a life without electricity. We don't have an outhouse or composting toilet, but one or the other will be needed if we totally disconnect.

No internet might be wonderful some day in the future, as people would no longer be looking at cellphones and ignoring life around them. It would mean the end of internet sales of products that I make and the end of easy banking, though. It was the primary concern when we bought our land, to have the best internet service. If you will need to be connected, you will have to go with the internet provider and physically visit your land to test the level of service.

In this stage of planning your escape, you will want to draw out the plan. It is fun! The house goes here and the storage building goes there. Draw it out. You will change it ten times, so just get started. Our cabin faces the valley with a big deck running all along the front. The driveway is a long, winding, steep road. The storage building is off to the side out of the way. We have parking places for vehicles, the side-by-side, and a place for the wood splitter and backhoe. Everything has a preferred location. After removing 25 trees we have space to park everything, finally. Originally it wasn't planned for at all. So, you see why it is important to think about the ideal place you are creating. Draw the gardens, raised garden beds, and fruit tree or grape growing areas. When you first start, you won't have all of this, but you want to scale and grow into the final plan. Dream big and start out practical.

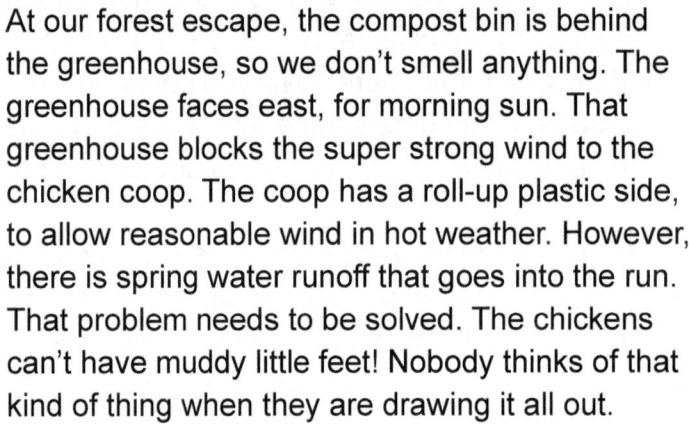

At our forest escape, the compost bin is behind the greenhouse, so we don't smell anything. The greenhouse faces east, for morning sun. That greenhouse blocks the super strong wind to the chicken coop. The coop has a roll-up plastic side, to allow reasonable wind in hot weather. However, there is spring water runoff that goes into the run. That problem needs to be solved. The chickens can't have muddy little feet! Nobody thinks of that kind of thing when they are drawing it all out.

Plan, using homestead web sites, and research what people say is best. Figure out your particular needs. Think about everything you might want and make a place for it. If you want duck eggs, then a duck pond must also go on your homestead layout. If you will need diesel or gasoline, plan an area for elevated gravity-fed tanks to store fuel.

The water source needs to be near your work area and home if you are not going to have municipal water. We have a spring that we can access for water, but it needs to be cleared out, and another area that appears to be a nice seep. We could drive that with a steel pipe, to get clear flowing water that doesn't stagnate. If we can't drive the pipe, we can install gravel around a pipe with holes drilled in it to remove the silt. Both of these sources are far from the cabin. It would be good exercise, if we need to carry that water daily. Are you going to collect rainwater for animals or chickens, for filtering for people to drink, or for gardening? Water storage is important, too. Plan an area for that. Think about the seasons and if that water storage might freeze.

Would you be installing electricity in your living quarters? Many states won't inspect your electric wiring panel box, until you have a sewage system that has been inspected and approved. That means no electricity in your home until you get the sewer installed. If you have an electric service hooked to a panel box in a storage building, then you have electricity on site that you could use. If you are not installing electric service, you may be using solar or a generator. Plan an area on the roof or in the field to have solar panels. Protect your generator from the elements but keep the exhaust fumes from going anywhere near your home. Remember, also, that the power company will clear cut a rather large swath of your forest to bring in those electric lines to your cabin. The right-of-way is supposed to be cut by the power company every six years, but we lose power frequently in storms, because trees are blowing into lines.

Waste disposal is a concern, so minimizing garbage is important. Composting and feeding safe scraps to chickens or pigs will get rid of most food waste. Paper items can be stored and used to start wood fires. Cardboard can be laid down in layers, in the bottom of raised garden beds, if you like permaculture. Glass jars can be used for hardware, chicken scratch, pasta, popcorn, lard, etc. Metal cans are great for storing fittings, tools, nuts, and bolts. Most everything can be upcycled or recycled.

When you plan for a certain level of dependency you feel comfortable with, also think about a future with full independence. We are still planning. We have a generator, but would also like solar. We have municipal water, but have cisterns to fall back on. We have a garden, but would love a trustworthy root cellar. We preserve food, but would like to learn fermenting. We have municipal water and also now have a water filtration unit, but we need to capture more rainfall. There is always something more that we want to include, in case we need to be off-grid entirely. It is a gradual mindset to become more and more independent. It is also a gradual accumulation of equipment that can help you live off-the-grid as a lifestyle choice or eventuality due to a national crisis. If we put Him first, God blesses us with many things. We step in faith and He takes it from there. Each time, He gives us more than we imagine possible.

We look around our homestead and ask ourselves what if what we have, is all we will ever have? If there is a crisis, could we survive without buying another thing? If we study 1800s living, we learn that they had few tools and supplies, but had survival knowledge. We need to establish a list of necessities and stock up on them, until we learn to be self-sufficient. We need backups for heat, electricity, and water sources.

If we have problems in our forest escape, we need a plan. If there are problems in nature, or in society, we need a plan. When we determine necessities, we need to run different scenarios to be proactive with solutions before the problem even happens. As it is, we have to be reactive to surprises that we didn't envision. That keeps us busy enough.

In the picture of the birds, to the right, you see three babies in the nest. There are really four in there - and that hidden one flew suddenly out into my camera and my face! It looks like they probably should have done it sooner, as they are pretty big to all be in that little nest under our porch roof. That baby took flight for the very first time!

Let the adventure begin!

*Matthew 6:26 Behold the fowls of the air: for they sow not,
neither do they reap, nor gather into barns; yet your heavenly Father feedeth them.
Are ye not much better than they?*

We really didn't think about how muddy the private road would be.

We were unable to use the road without load after load of gravel. It was about $3,000 worth of gravel, at first. Then, again in three years.

Chapter 5 – The Land of the Free

Romans 12:2 And be not conformed to this world: but be ye transformed by the renewing of your mind, that ye may prove what is that good, and acceptable, and perfect, will of God.

How many people will be with you, and how much land do you need? Do you have water and elevation to avoid flooding? Is the forest able to produce wood for heating? Is it affordable?

> **1 Corinthians 7:22-23**
> For he that is called in the Lord, being a servant, is the Lord's freeman: likewise also he that is called, being free, is Christ's servant. 23 Ye are bought with a price; be not ye the servants of men.

You are thinking of breaking away from the city, developments, or suburbs. Maybe you don't like the way society is changing. You don't need to conform to this world. Follow God's will for your life. See what your choices are for the future. Freedom in rural living is finding land that is perfect for your needs and homesteading as much as you choose, on that land. You can withdraw into a lifestyle that is more wholesome and centered around God.

When choosing land, consider the slope of the land, the forest, and if there is a water source that you can access or not. You need a flat area to build your homestead on. You need a clearing to have trees a good distance from many areas you will develop. We didn't clear out enough trees as we wanted to keep almost all of them. Years later, we removed 25 trees from around our cabin. Our main goal was to have privacy and to have enough affordable land to be separate from any other people living in the area. Trees grow quickly, blow down in storms, and give squirrels a bridge to our roof. We need to cut down six trees in the garden, now. We really didn't think about how muddy the private road would be – until we were unable to use the road without load after load of gravel. It was about $3,000 worth of gravel. Think about the equipment you may need if you choose a challenging location.

Do the extensive research needed to find land, over a long period of time. This is something you may look for over the course of many months. We explored the state of our choice, Kentucky, in multiple trips, and in many hours of research online.

We chose the state due to the people and the values they have, the low taxes, and their respect for The Constitution of the United States of America.

Consider utilities. Internet access was needed for my work. We could not live in the mountainous eastern regions, due to the lack of utilities in place. We found land west of the mountains where most utilities were in place, or could be installed. Municipal water was not available on our parcel of land. Our neighbors had lived 11 years using cisterns, so land without a water well is possible to live on. You would need a tank and a truck to haul the water. Water wells were out of the question in this location, due to natural contaminants from the underground cave systems.

Buy more land than you think you will need. More land and less house is good advice, if you like privacy and want to expand your homestead. You can always add on to your home when you have the money to do so. With land, it may not be possible to buy more acreage around your property. For us, 43 acres proved to be the right amount, and with logging roads we can drive through the property with a side-by-side UTV Utility Task Vehicle, or all-terrain vehicle ATV.

Consider if the positioning of your home on the land and think about security as well. If things turn ugly and there is unrest in our country, how safe would you be? Build on the hill, with natural perimeters or future fences and gates. Plan on being able to lock people out, and lock up your belongings.

> If you are short on money, you can look for short-term land contracts with a deed, a promissory note with a deed, owner financing, or a self-directed IRA, or other creative financial arrangements. Make sure a lawyer looks at the agreement and that you ideally get a deed with your name on it, before building and investing money in the land.

The property deed proves that you own the land and it is recorded in the courthouse. When the loan against the deed is paid in full, then the lien is released against the property and that also is recorded in the courthouse.

Mineral rights are also something you want to ask about. The land should come with the oil and gas rights, but you need to make sure, if this is important for your future.

Legally, ensure that the land you are buying is free and clear, as well as what you need for your homestead. Have your attorney make sure the land you are thinking of buying has ingress (coming in) and egress (going out) or an easement in writing. Make sure

nobody has an easement or right-of-way through your prospective land, because you don't want people driving through your property, either. Make sure the land is not land-locked. The property must have a way in and out, or you can't use it. You need to be able to drive to your land legally, and to come and go freely. Look at the quality and types of trees. See if you have a water source, or any evidence of flooding. Make sure you have a copy of the land survey, and physically walk the land, to get a feel for the topography or hills and valleys, the neighbors, etc., before you purchase the land. This is vital.

Chapter 6 – Determine Necessities

Hebrews 13:5 Let your conversation be without covetousness; and be content with such things as ye have: for he hath said, I will never leave thee, nor forsake thee.

What tools, equipment, vehicles, farm implements, garden supplies, food or clothing will you need?

Remember, you don't need everything all at once. Basic home, auto and gardening tools will be adequate. Think about the operations in advance. You probably would be building, chopping, cutting, digging, and splitting. If you will be building a cabin, you need power tools and hand tools for construction. You would need the power screwdriver, circular saw and drill. We immediately bought a miter saw for cutting so many boards. Yard sales are great for gathering tools you need; since they are used, they are super cheap. A $30 shovel could be $5, so this is a real savings. It will be important to buy a quality measuring tape.

> Whatever you purchase, buy in bulk because in six months the costs could be almost double. Think about hardware – buckets of screws instead of boxes – to save money. Supplies are like stock market traded commodities. The prices go up and down and can be so volatile. Lumber can be low one month and 4X as much the next. Waiting to purchase until the price goes down is something we have learned is very helpful. Most projects can wait a little.

Make your lists in advance and try to save gasoline by making less trips to the home improvement store, the hardware store or the farm supply store. It saves you time and money to carefully plan in advance.

For me, in the middle of the blackness of night, the power company sensor light was a necessary item. The light comes on at dusk and turns off at dawn. For as long as the electrical grid works and we can afford to have municipal electricity, I will have the outdoor floodlight. We also have LED sensor lights on all sides of the house.

Keep a master list of the "some day" items you really want, but don't need today. Each month, you might be able to buy one of those items, as well. Our "some day" items become less and less with each passing year. It feels good to finally get something you have been waiting a long time for. We appreciate those things so much! For me, I'm thinking it would be nice to get a good meat grinder soon, but they are pretty expensive, so I am looking at yard sales for one of the vintage ones without too much wear and tear. The new ones look pretty fragile and the vintage ones are still around and good, so the materials used were much better in the past.

Basic garden tools include the hoe, spade, shovel, and metal rake. If you want a bulk, it might make life easier. If you are working with raised beds, then turning the soil with a machine is not necessary. The wheelbarrow is worth investing in for moving dirt, rocks, feed, etc. It is also useful to have a hatchet.

The chicken coop tools at a minimum include a square shovel for cleaning, scoops, and food-grade buckets with lids to hold the feed and scratch. Water tubs of some type are vital, as well.

Coop and run materials are important to price out. You can get started with hardware cloth, hardware for doors and treated lumber.

A good fence is worth investing in, so consider the T poles and welded wire fencing of maybe 100 feet to get started. You would want a gate too, so there are more treated boards and hinges to buy. It would be advised to buy a fence post pounder and a 5-pound hammer or a sledgehammer, as well.

If you have roads to maintain, it might mean using heavy equipment. After a while, you may buy a tractor, bulldozer, or a backhoe. You can always borrow or rent big equipment if you need it.

Make sure you have the insect repellent, hornet spray, a sewing kit and a good first aid kit.

If you plan to plant big fields in large crops, you will need the tractor and farm implements. You need to till and disc, and if you have a brush hog and a grader, those are also great attachments to accumulate as soon as possible for maintaining fields, trails and roads. Having extra hoses and clamps, oil and hydraulic fluid on hand is a good idea. Fuel storage for diesel is also nice, but expensive. We would love to have an elevated tank for this. It is on the "someday list". For now, a few cans of gasoline and diesel are good enough. I also keep my truck full, so this actually serves as a gasoline reserve for us.

Hoses and buckets and Y fittings are needed, but be sure to do your research in buying them as most will not stand the test of time or endure harsh winters. Figure on leaks and get the mending hardware to mend the hoses. Those cheap plastic fittings last six months. A good, large watering can is also nice.

In terms of food, water, paper goods including toilet paper, and emergency supplies, you want to plan to have a large quantity on hand. This means you won't have to leave often to fetch, and in bad weather or emergencies you want to be able to stay home. To start, a month of supplies will be good but you want to work toward six months if possible. This means potable water and canned goods, as well as a stocked freezer. If you can buy a new freezer, they are really efficient. Ours says it costs $26 per year to run, which is a whole lot cheaper than the old ones used to cost to operate.

If you have pets, flocks and herds, you need to keep that stocked up food dry and away from pests. I do keep my chicken feed in the greenhouse, in food-safe buckets, so it is handy since I don't have a barn. It also isn't very far to walk with heavy buckets, or jugs of water in the winter.

With children, there are considerations that might be different than with adults only in the forest escape. Children need to bathe daily, to check for ticks and insect bites, as well as to wash completely. Kids eat a lot, so extra

snacks and juice, etc. would need to be planned for, as well as the storage space for those items. Shelves up along the ceiling area can go all around a room. You might like to have the small garden tools, too, so they can help at any age. Kids need drink bottles, and straw hats or something to protect their head if they are in the sun all day. If they hold chickens and gather eggs, they must wash their hands. Also, it can't be all about work, so play time, hide and seek, and blowing bubbles or making s'mores around the bonfire are important. The homestead must be clear of rusty nails, hornet nests, and anything that is a safety concern for kids.

If you have a wood stove, then you might cook on the top of it, or boil water for coffee or tea. The teapot is really useful. It is also necessary to keep water on top of the wood stove when it is burning, to keep humidity in the home.

If you work outdoors, you need practical well-made clothing. I always wear layers, such as a T-shirt, extra roomy sweatshirt, and a hoodie. You need a work jacket with pockets, leather gloves and a hat for winter and a hat and sunglasses for summer. A good raincoat is indispensable. Good garden boots or chicken boots are nice - not too heavy but protect from wet conditions and other stuff. Consider your seasons, so if you have a tough winter, you need long underwear and warm winter boots and heavier gear. Make sure you have lots of pockets or a tool belt or fanny pack. Those things come in handy.

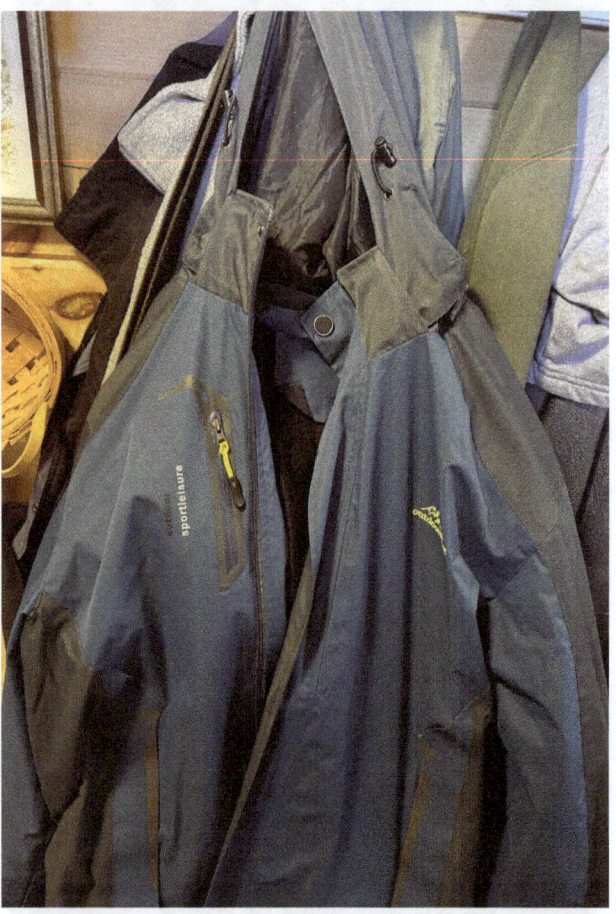

> You can start to get a mental image now, regarding what might be considered extra items and items that might be considered necessities. Each homesteader has a different idea of what they need. If you forget something, chances are that a neighbor will let you borrow it.

Heating with wood, you will want a good chain saw, oil, fuel and spare chains/bars, and a chain sharpener.

The generator is really necessary, and the dual fuel is a better choice.

There are basic necessities we need. Fire extinguishers are necessary, as are smoke detectors, so spend the money and ensure your safety. A shop vacuum is really important, as it is non-stop mess getting started, as well as maintaining everything. Matches, a torch, lighters, rope, wire and a pulley could prove useful. Think about repairs you might have to make. Fittings, hardware, clamps, and wire ties are good to have on hand. Everyone should have a hand saw and a hacksaw. Tarps and bungee cords will be needed. A nice workbench in a back room or in a storage building is pretty nice, too. Tire repair, auto fluids and additives are good to buy and stock up on.

You can build a wood holder or lean-to in order to shelter your wood long term. If you are splitting by hand and don't have a wood splitter, then you will need to buy the sledge hammer and wedges.

Think about transporting and hauling things. A good, used side-by-side vehicle or ATV with a trailer could make life easier in terms of hauling materials, equipment, or water. Loan payments would be lower on used equipment. The side-by-side is our most used and most valued piece of equipment. Dollies or hand trucks help you move heavy objects. Some things, even with help, you just can't move without some kinds of equipment. The backhoe was needed to unload the wood stove from the truck. The dolly was used to bring the wood stove into the house.

The air compressor provides power to the staple gun, fills your tires and so much more. It is okay to buy the smaller one as it does most anything you need.

Communication of some type is important, so maybe having a cell phone even if it is a burner phone. If there is no internet or cell tower, maybe a land line would be needed. Until you are up and running at least, work on the safe side.

Everyone has different ideas of what necessities are, so you may need other items.

Chapter 7 – Homestead in Nature

Matthew 7:24-25 Therefore whosoever heareth these sayings of mine, and doeth them, I will liken him unto a wise man, which built his house upon a rock: And the rain descended, and the floods came, and the winds blew, and beat upon that house; and it fell not: for it was founded upon a rock.

Draw out the land with house, cisterns, outhouse, garages, buildings, storage, animal pens, wood racks, gardens, raised garden beds, coops and greenhouses.

Your homestead will be built in nature. You will be in nature's domain, so you play by nature's rules. Nature is beautiful, but powerful. Consider the sunrise and sunset, think about the wind direction and strength, and plan for rain and erosion, as well as ice and snow.

Situate everything for expansion, correction, or growth. Trees should not be too close to dwellings, even though they are so pretty and wonderful. Hot sun without shade trees can be an issue. Think about the wind in each season. Maybe the doors to the buildings need to open in a particular direction, so your door doesn't get ripped off, or hit you really hard when you go in and out of buildings in high winds.

Certainly don't build in a valley near a river, as flooding will be an issue. As in our case, we are on a high hill with a winding road and steep terrain: this means that in icy conditions we don't leave. Of course, when we were planning the house location, we just thought about privacy. Reality comes quickly, and you learn with experience.

Coyotes, mountain lions and bears can come within a mile or less of your home, but that only happens around here once every three years or so. Predatory animals want to be away from people for the most part. If you live in a way that does not encourage wild animals to visit, then all should be fine. That means not leaving food out or have a garbage dump by your home. If you think about what might attract a wild animal, you want to avoid that. Chickens in an enclosed run are better than free-ranging chickens if you live in an area where a lot of coyotes roam frequently.

Ice is heavy and coats everything, so trees bend or break, and electric wires come down. The birds need food in the bitter cold, but especially when there is a coating of ice that is nearly 1/4" thick.

Sometimes, nature blocks your way home. It was a blessing this tree did not hit the backhoe, garden fence, fire pit or the house.

This wood is not great for burning, so we will use it for other things.

Simply sketch a layout that you feel might work for individual components of your homestead. Then, envision the whole layout of the land where you will develop those parts. When you see the big picture, you will have a plan for growth. It starts out small, but then it expands. It is better to plan out those phases of development. We might not

ever have a workshop, pond, or a barn, but it is nice to think about where they would go, if we decided to build them.

Consider practical items. You could plan rain water collection off of your roofs. You could have gravity-fed fuel tanks. You could broom out your barn down into a gully where you compost.

Plan for bigger areas than you imagine. You might build smaller and then want to enlarge the structure in the future.

Chapter 7 - Homestead in Nature

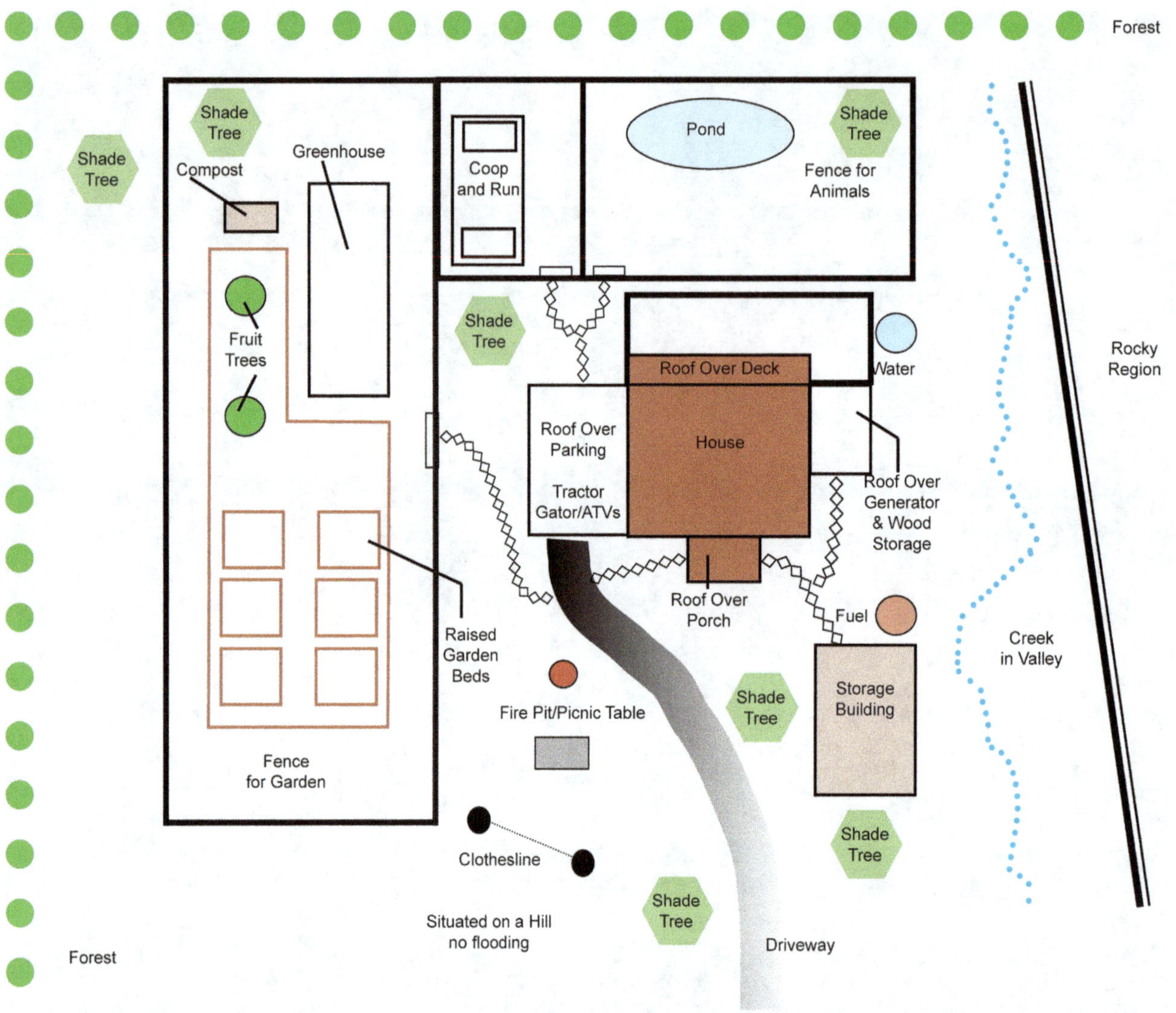

Insects are a concern. We have ticks and it is necessary to use insect repellent. Black widows and brown recluse spiders live here. Bees can be troublesome. Every year ants march in and gnats come calling. It is a phase and normal each year. There are natural concoctions that can be made to help with each pest.

Nature provides many opportunities to learn, supplies to use and adventures to enjoy. Leaves are good for composting, tree branches are great for kindling, and trees are great for firewood. If you have a pond or river, you can go fishing. If you enjoy birdwatching, photography, or painting, you can enjoy these hobbies every day!

Squirrels are incredible pests and leap onto the roof or crawl up the exterior walls, run across railings, and scoot across the porches. I have heard that you can eat squirrels and if times were tough, we would never be without food! We had a gray squirrel get inside the cabin and it was a 5-pounder that attacked the dog and caused a very big circus inside the house. They can be thought of as cute, but they can be destructive,

chewing cables, wires and basically anything that they are determined to chew. If you come from the city, no worries, just imagine those large urban rats that you encounter. City rats or rural squirrels - not a big difference. Of course, rats don't rain down acorns, out of the trees, onto your metal roof. That is a special kind of annoying, I promise!

Trees fall, roads flood, winds blow, and seasons come and go. Think about where you place your buildings, and how you will walk to do your chores. During the tornado season you can have straight-line winds and hurricane force winds, as well. Thank God, the fallen tree from the last storm missed the backhoe, the fire pit and the garden fence, as well as the house. It was perfect placement to do the least amount of damage. I was not going in the garden gate when the huge tree branch fell and crunched the chain link fence and garden gate. Thank you, God!

Chapter 8 – Ask for and Accept God's Blessings

1 Peter 1:7 That the trial of your faith, being much more precious than of gold that perisheth, though it be tried with fire, might be found unto praise and honour and glory at the appearing of Jesus Christ:

Ask God in prayer to show you what to do and look for confirmation that you know His will in a direction for your life.

We are not in control, and we do not make our world. God is in control. The lifestyle choice is accepting all of God's blessings and trusting Him to help us. We step in faith and discover the blessings God has for us!

Mark 10:15 Verily I say unto you, Whosoever shall not receive the kingdom of God as a little child, he shall not enter therein.

There are Christian concepts that people talk about, but rarely put into practice as a way of life. So many people sit on the fence and they don't establish which side they are on. It also means that sometimes they do nothing.

The modern church seems quite political in a way that isn't dealing with world politics so much, but more internal politics. People are so busy telling others what to do and being that particular ideal church-approved Christian that they forget the love of Christ. It is more like churchianity than Christianity. They have forgotten their first love. It isn't the case with all churches, but if this is the Laodicean church age, Jesus is not happy with our way of worshipping, pastoring, or living. If you look around at what people are all busy doing, it isn't necessarily what glorifies the Father in Heaven. In some cases, it is putting more emphasis on the church process and rules internally. Movement isn't progress. Being busy isn't growth. Some pastors seem quite concerned with tithes and are not walking the walk, though they talk the talk. I heard comments online from major pastors that if they spoke of a certain doctrine it would split the church in two and the tithes would be less. Shocking. Some pastors don't want free eggs donated to give to people who are in need. We wanted to help feed people. I am not sure pastors know how poor some people are, and that a free breakfast would be much appreciated! Maybe some pastors are not reaching the ones who are truly lost, in need and suffering. Some pastors just focus on those who tithe the most.

Let's ask God for His blessings, and when we receive those blessings, do the most we can with them! Let's be that light for Christ and help everyone we can. As we separate from the society that is going in the wrong direction, we will be stronger as we study at home, with the Holy Spirit as our guide on a daily basis.

If we love God as children, then we think of Him as our Father in Heaven. We know He loves us, and we can come to him for anything and everything! Let's just break it down that simply. In such innocence, let's just start over from today forward. There is no need to look back. Trust and obey.

God wants us to minister to Him, needs us to love Him, desires that we accept Jesus as our Savior, and wants us to realize that our lives are for His purpose. When we come to this understanding, what about saturating ourselves in this modern society is wholesome? There is so much more to life! Why do we want to be distracted? We can focus on a daily walk in peace. It is about surrender to the will of God. When we do that, we ask for certain things and when we get them, we need to use them - whatever those blessings might be! Also, whatever persecution there might be. And, despite whatever attack Satan launches against us as well. We can't be timid in doing what we are called or led to do.

Watch for the blessings from God and listen to the small, still voice of the Holy Spirit. If we don't pay attention we can miss something. Don't worry, the Holy Spirit will repeat the message and will put a burden on your heart to obey. We accept the gifts and the leading from God and we do our best. Through the Holy Spirit, we can do great things for God, using the blessings he bestows upon us. Whatever we do, it is not from our strength: it is from God's strength.

The blessings we have experienced are so many that we have trouble remembering them all. I started the prayer journal, so I would not forget.

I so wanted pine trees where the land was barren from the electric company clearing for the poles and wires to be installed. I thought maybe 20 or 30 would be so pretty. Today, there are probably 300 in that area. It is simply beautiful. God did that. We always are given more than we ask for.

> *Luke 12:48*
> *But he that knew not, and did commit things worthy of stripes, shall be beaten with few stripes. For unto whomsoever much is given, of him shall be much required: and to whom men have committed much, of him they will ask the more.*

We are given things that we don't even ask for, because God knows what we need.

Whether you choose your forest escape as a refuge to return home to after a long work day, or you live and work at home full-time, you will see God's many blessings on a daily basis. When my husband was working full-time, prior to retirement, he was in a hurry to get home and stay there. I worked at home all day and wanted to be off and running somewhere, back then. Now, we are in tune and prefer to be in our forest escape more than anywhere else.

> **A forest escape is escaping from the chaos of society but it is more of a transition to a place of peace with God. It is a place where we are more apt to pray, to see the answers to prayers, and to be thankful for each and every blessing. I think we are also more aware that the Holy Spirit is in us, also.**

God wants to give His children so many blessings, and He wants to know what you will do with them. If you are given more, then more is expected. So, will you share what you have been given? You could teach others, you could share the fruits of your labor, or you could be an example for others, shining the light of Christ and showing the love of God.
You could share the Gospel with everyone you interact with, including friends, family, colleagues and neighbors.

We asked God for a quiet place and a refuge, and it has turned into so much more! We learn new things daily. We study and research to see what other homesteaders are doing. We try to accomplish things that work great, and others fail miserably. It is trial and error to see what works for each person. Sharing this life with family is so nice. Kids of all ages love baby chicks. Everyone loves fresh eggs and vegetables from the homestead.

If we don't keep track of everything, we will forget it quickly. There are things we were so sure we would never forget, but we have. If you find really good information, it is wise to print it out and save it in a 3-ring binder. For the future, you have a reference library and can look up what to do with a poisonous snake bite, a case of poison ivy, or what gets rid of worms on tomatoes, etc. The information is complete because you have researched the topics and continue to build this library of resources. I have the topics indexed and in a particular order. As I find nice articles or diagrams, I print them out, and add them to the proper binder. Of course I have a big tub of filing, so not everything is in the proper binder yet. Kids and grandchildren can help with the task of sorting information and hole punching the binder pages. Also, the grandchildren bring little flowers when they visit and we share quality time. As they get older, they are more and more helpful. This information is stored for them.

It is most important to pursue this lifestyle and this quality of life for the next generations. We have done so many wonderful things, but most of what we do is for the adult children and their children, so that generations know how to live simply, have their priorities in order, and worship God in their own way. We want them to have that opportunity to flourish, to be healthy, and to have hope.

Books regarding indoor gardening, making pemmican, home-made medicines, and mushrooming are all great books to have in your bookcase. I never read novels or adventure stories, now. I only study the Bible, books on Bible studies, and homesteading types of books to learn what I need to know.

I don't really have time for entertainment and I don't really find a need to "escape" since I am living in my forest escape and I am actually very happy. It is amazing how people change and embrace their way of life when it is in balance and built with their own hands. We know that it is by the grace of God that all has been bestowed upon us.

I want to be sure all people, from all walks of life and all struggles get mentioned in this book. We have talked about people who are under corporate life stress, those who are or were in the military, moms who want to stay home with kids, those who are ignored by pastors, and those who are poor. I want to point this out, also, to anyone who is dependent or was dependent on various substances. People use food, drugs, alcohol, video games and so many things to escape "real" life because their life is hard, hopeless or hurtful. Anyone who pursues the forest escape is going to feel like they have escaped all of those problems that had gotten them down. It will be a victory through Jesus, and it will be easy to forget the old destructive habits. Nature, healthy food, learning new things, and working hard help a person stay on a healthy track.

It is important to realize that God protects us, but He expects us to do our part. We can't be lazy and expect everything to drop in our lap. We need to work. We need to perform the will of God. We need to follow His leading.

Our last home had a running creek all year long.

Chapter 9 – Water in All Seasons

John 4:14 But whosoever drinketh of the water that I shall give him shall never thirst; but the water that I shall give him shall be in him a well of water springing up into everlasting life.

Water is the most important daily requirement that must be met for people, plants, flocks, and animals. Quality water resources, a water well, water filtration and cisterns should be considered.

John 4:13-14 Jesus answered and said unto her, Whosoever drinketh of this water shall thirst again: 14 But whosoever drinketh of the water that I shall give him shall never thirst; but the water that I shall give him shall be in him a well of water springing up into everlasting life.

Keep in mind that the spiritual water of life is most important and Jesus tells us that we will never thirst again when we come to His living waters. First read the Word of God, and all else follows.

An artesian well brings groundwater to the surface because it is under pressure within the aquifer.

A driven well is cased, but it may be contaminated easily because it draws water from surface aquifers.

Drilled wells access water from aquifers below the surface. A water well driller can drill down hundreds or thousands of feet in depth and the well requires the installation of casing. Kentucky water may have natural contaminants, so it was cost-prohibitive for us, at approximately $10,000 with no guarantee of drinkable water.

Natural springs are higher volume; formed when groundwater flows to the surface. It usually happens when the water table is at surface level.

Seeps are like springs, but lower volume, and mostly occur in lower elevations where water runs downhill. You can dig where there is wet ground and possibly get water.

Creeks are natural streams of water normally smaller than rivers, and often are tributaries to a river.

Rainwater can be collected as it falls and kept in a rain barrel with a screen to prevent leaves from getting in the water.

Our property did not have a well or municipal water. We hauled water for three years in a tank in the back of a truck. It required two loads each weekend, to fill the two 275-gallon plastic food safe tanks that served as our water cisterns. This system provided water for showering, the toilet and for washing.

Our property finally did get municipal water. The water meter was placed 1,000 feet from our home.

We borrowed a backhoe and my husband dug the ditch to the proper

depth and I placed the water line in that trench. We had use of the backhoe for a short time. We barely ate and we didn't sleep all through the night. We both had to work in the morning.

I finished the last water line placement in the morning, after I worked for a while online. During that next morning placement I was so tired and I became entangled in the roots of a big tree down in the trench. I tipped over, fell flat on my back and was covered over in muddy roots and laid there crying real tears. I would have normally laughed, but I was just so tired and it felt like being in a SciFi movie where a person is caught by some alien growth and can't move. That was physical and mental exhaustion. I was so overwhelmed at the idea of

having water at our home and that was a good thing. However, the physical exhaustion was too much at that point. I did finally get up out of the ditch, cleaned off, and put the last bit of water line in the trench, despite all the roots.

It was such a tiring project, but we finally had municipal water after three long years of hauling water. We covered the water line ditch and then hooked up the connection to the house.

Water storage is also important and needs to be insulated, heated, or in a building in the winter. There are additives that can be put in the water to keep it long-term. Gravity fed means positioning storage tanks at a higher elevation to get water to your home with pressure for showering or washing. A camping shower bag is good to have.

If we want to be off-grid, we have springs that could be developed more and used, and we could collect rainwater. Research rain barrels.

The property has multiple springs that can be exposed, dug out and cleaned up. Each year my husband increases the size of the water pooling areas, and the animals sure appreciate accessible water in the hot summer months. Eventually, if needed, these will be sources for our drinking water. Some of the water seems to be coming out of a layer of quartz, and it looks crystal clear. We will need to have it tested, to see if it is safe without filtration. Otherwise, we

do have a filtration unit that we bought and really love. There are a lot of sites out there, some veteran-owned, and they also have emergency food with a 25-year shelf life. You can look up survival sites, homesteading, preppers and off-the-grid living, to get information regarding products from people who have tried them firsthand. We add the mined mineral salt to our water.

Filtration could be an important aspect of being independent, in the future, or if you choose to live off-the-grid. Many survival sites sell filtration units that filter out 200 or so contaminants, so there are certainly choices for getting safe drinking water. It is important to have an extra stock of filters, which probably will have to be purchased over time, as they are very expensive.

If you tap into a water source, your could buy a hand pump or hydrant, to get the water up out of the ground and into an area where you need to use the water.

Stainless steel buckets are great for storing and carrying water, or for feeding pets and livestock. Stainless cleans up nice, won't rust, and causes no negative taste.

Chapter 10 – The Home of the Brave

Psalms 91:1-2 He that dwelleth in the secret place of the most High shall abide under the shadow of the Almighty. I will say of the Lord, He is my refuge and my fortress: my God; in him will I trust.

The home you choose could be a tiny home, a shipping container, a log home, an Amish-built cabin, or so many other choices that you can imagine.

Your cabin or main home building can be inexpensive, but well planned it can serve more purpose. If you extend a roof, you have firewood storage. If your house is up off the ground, then there can be storage or a root cellar underneath.

The initial cabin will prove to be inadequate over time and you will wish you chose different options, so plan for this in advance. Tiny might be nice, but what if someone visits and wants to sleep over? What if the weather is bad and you go stir crazy due to not enough space? Where will it go if you want to install a wood stove later?

Inside, you have options and possibly those options will need to change or expand. Is the electrical wiring going to be simple? Consider how water goes through the living space to the kitchen and the bathroom, how to keep pipes from freezing, and maybe provide water for outdoor use.

CABIN

I always wanted to be an architect, and I am thankful for the opportunity to have one home that I could design. I drew the plans for our 2-story forest escape cabin with a gambrel roof. The floor plan was drawn eight times, to be right for our lifestyle. The bathroom is quite large for a small cabin, and we have two offices upstairs, so each of us has a workspace with a door. The loft is not big, but the open ceiling in the dining room and living room are pretty and let in a lot of light. I plan to enjoy reading the Bible and drinking tea on that loft one winter day, while watching the wood stove fire below.

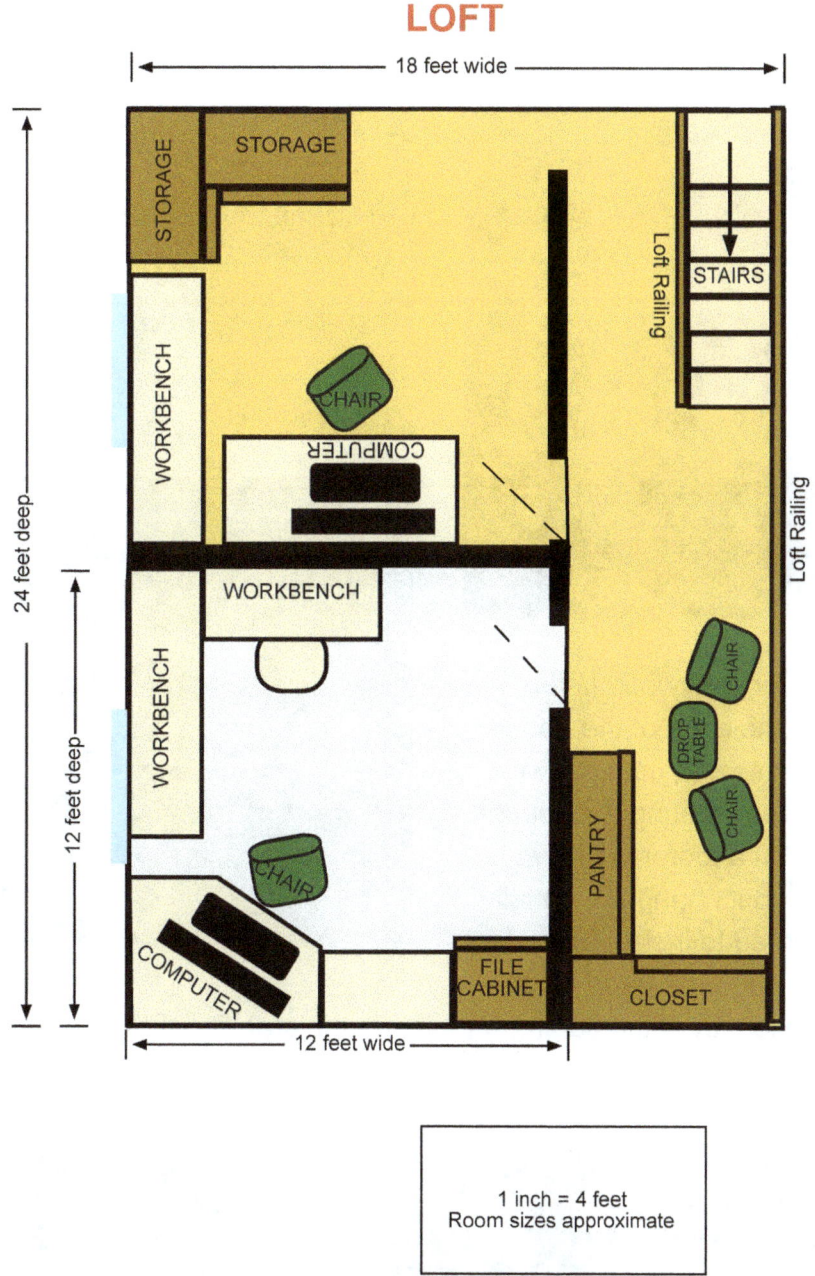

Imagine your home, the traffic pattern and what rooms you would like. Draw it out, so you can experiment with what you want for living quarters.

When it was time to build, we chose to combine skills and tasks to build our forest cabin. We decided to ask the Amish to help us in building the exterior of our cabin. This was a low expense compared to prices today, and we should have probably spent a bit more.

The Amish built the exterior and the second-floor platform inside. The roof is metal and the siding is board and batten. I have a couple of regrets, as the metal roofing should

have been put over a plywood layer for strength, and the ends of the house should have been sealed up tight, with proper squirrel-proof venting. A cabin on stilts rather than on a footer is probably not the best idea, but cheap. Thankfully, the builders returned to install concrete pads with blocking to hold three steel beams the entire length of the cabin, to maintain the stability of the home, because the original stilts were not quite the right size or spacing for a two-story building on a hill.

Over the course of 38 days we built the interior including room partitions, plumbing and electrical wiring, to the point where we could move in. At that point, we had appliances in the kitchen, and a functioning bathroom. We celebrated the first time the toilet could be flushed using jugs of water in the toilet tank! Small things became cause to celebrate. The flooring was a mix of

what was on sale and what would be durable. Some rooms didn't get any flooring other than the OSB, initially. My office still has carpet over OSB. One day, I will put in the hardwood flooring.

The laws are different in each state and it depends on the number of acres that you buy, as to whether or not you need permits. Installing certain aspects of the home are contingent upon other items being done first. For instance, we could not have the electricity hooked up until the sewer was installed. That was a strange concept to us, but I guess the state wants to ensure that homes have a working septic system. If a person wants electricity then they will install the septic system.

Cash from selling our New York home and belongings was the only money used for the cabin build. We did not want a mortgage. It was not easy, and the work stopped from no available cash multiple times, and many projects were left undone.

The cabin initially had two cisterns underneath, with plumbing to the electric water pump, which provided the laundry, kitchen and bathroom the necessary water. We hauled water in the back of the truck for three years, until we got municipal water.

Outside, the cabin has weather protection including a long front covered deck facing the valley, with a fenced in area for the dog, and a small, covered porch to enter the cabin from the driveway.

We enclosed the bottom of the house, covering the stilts, to protect the floors from wind and to also keep the water lines and cisterns from freezing. In the under house area, we could build a root cellar. The location would be convenient and the humidity would be perfect.

We also built a lean-to roof over the generator and covered it with 12ml reinforced greenhouse plastic. It is possible to store more firewood and fuel cans there as well. Always think about protection from the elements. Tarps do not last very long, so buy the best ones or invest in the 12 mil reinforced greenhouse plastic tarps with grommets.

The front porch should have been a bit bigger, but it was a last-minute, wonderful decision to add it and money was limited. It does hold two buckets of salt and a shovel, in the winter, so it is sufficient.

Chapter 10 - The Home of the Brave

We have no closets, and in retrospect I would say that was a mistake. I have learned that storage is vital. If I could do it over today, I would have whole walls of cupboards, with shelves, too.

The washer and dryer are under the stairs to the loft, to save space. The Amish builders measured and figured the best way to build the stairway to accommodate the appliances. I built little shelves out of scrap wood that I could find, and those shelves hold cleaning supplies, laundry soap, insect repellent, and insecticides, as well as some automotive fluids.

We have shelves in many places, such as over my workbench in my office. I learned to make corbel supports for shelves, as buying them was extremely expensive. Each corbel was selling for $60. It was easy to make them with the miter saw and staple gun. The cheap floral print boxes on the shelves hold all kinds of things, look less messy, and keep things organized.

I built cubbies in the entry way, using the staple gun and that was a mistake because the staples come out of the wood easily. I had to add screws for strength.

On the loft we assembled an affordable armoire and a bookcase, and a 12-cube

shelf with cloth baskets for storage.

In the bathroom, simple shelves hold towels, and a bench for sitting after a shower has space underneath for a stockpile of hand soap, shampoo, conditioner, hand sanitizer, mouthwash, and more.

Chapter 10 - The Home of the Brave

We lived seven years without our wished-for pine tongue and groove walls, so all of that time we were looking at plastic sheeting over insulation and studs.

When we finally were able to afford the wood for the walls, the look of the cabin interior was transformational! We had some other Amish builders work on a lot of the really high ceilings, and some other rooms. The light of the pine was so pretty! The brown insulation paper had been so dark and dreary, compared to the new sweet glow of white pine!

I literally cried to see the cabin finally look like we imagined – better than we imagined.

Looking from the loft it is possible to see the interior finally without construction tools everywhere.

The flooring was a fun project. We used yellow pine and placed that down over underlayment. We did not stain the wood in our bedroom. It is very light and airy. In my husband's office, we stained it a dark color, but in the kitchen, hallway and entry way we stained an old antique look with stain cloths from the home improvement store. You can literally paint your look as you like. Then, we coated the floors with three layers of polyurethane and it had to be the kind that doesn't smell horrible and dries

really fast. That was kind of a tedious task, but well worth the effort.
Spice storage and stainless steel pan storage is above the stove. One shelf is a really pretty piece of cedar wood. The rest is pine.

Our oldest son and his wife helped us build the interior of the home, for months, over the course of five different trips down to Kentucky to help us.

Three years after we moved to Kentucky, our oldest son, his wife, and their baby moved to Kentucky, to begin their forest escape. It was an opportunity for his wife to be a stay-at-home mom, and a higher-paying job for him.

Their house in New York did not sell right away, so they lived with us for two years and eight months. We never fought. We knew this was a dream coming true and we would have family, which is most important. During that time, their second son was born. He was born in our living room, in a birthing pool of warm water, with the nicest midwife present. God's protection and blessing has been continual.

After helping us build our cabin, they opted for a different style of home and workshop on the gated 13 acres that we gave them in exchange for all that work.

Our oldest son and his wife and two boys now have their own home, but it was a privilege to share our lives in the home we built together. It was a circus most of the time and we had so many pets all in one house, toys and babies, and so much laundry! It was not always easy but it was so worth it all. I still cry when I think how God worked it all out.

Our youngest son returned from his

military service and stayed in our cabin for a year helping us with projects, before moving to Seattle, WA. Then he moved to South Korea, for two years, to be near his wife's family. Finally he, his wife, and their twins moved to Kentucky, about an hour away from us. His wife is a stay-at-home mom, too. The kids benefit so much from this.

It is such a wonderful thing to share family times, for the first time ever! Our youngest son joined the military as a junior in high school, in the delayed enlistment program, so we did not have family time very often over the course of many years.

> Our home is the home that love built: God's love made it possible. The love and hard work of family made it a physical reality. From the family help moving out of the NY house and into a moving truck, through the process to the current day, family love made it happen.

When you think about the home you might build, you will need to think about family times and having spaces for being together, cooking and maybe spending the night. What if there was a crisis? Could you house other family members who need help?

Also consider fuel for everyday living. If you are off-grid, you won't have electricity, unless you have a generator with fuel, or solar power with panels, inverter, batteries, meter and electric panel.

If you have electricity, then it will make life easier, but you also need to think about heat. You can heat with electric, propane, wood pellets, wood log stove, fuel oil and more. Research the choices, and see what is good for you.

We have talked about building a gasifier, like they used in WWII. Gasifiers burn wood chips, sawdust, charcoal or coal to provide electricity for furnaces, cooking, stoves and for some vehicles.

As you encounter various types of situations, you will think more in terms of backups for everything. It isn't so much about quantity but more about alternatives. Think about Plan A, Plan B and Plan C.

Chapter 10 - The Home of the Brave Page 75

Chapter 11 – Food to Eat and for the Soul

Amos 8:11 Behold, the days come, saith the Lord God, that I will send a famine in the land, not a famine of bread, nor a thirst for water, but of hearing the words of the Lord:

Nourish the body and the soul. When you nourish the soul, you read the Word of God, pray to your Father in Heaven, and thank Him for all things. It would be nice to invite neighbors for home Bible studies, prayer meetings, and to talk about God's blessings. Nobody pressures you to stop, or persecutes you for being a Christian. When you nourish the body, you eat what is good and you can control your food quality, omit chemicals and growth hormones, and experience new and different foods! You make a lifestyle choice that allows you to do this. You can embrace what is good, and good for you!

God makes the garden grow. We try our best to grow vegetables and fruits, but maybe (like me) it isn't your best skill. I still stare at seeds that sprout into seedlings and am amazed at God's great power and plan for us. The tiniest of things are so amazing that I am just in awe. I have prayed for the greenhouse plants and the garden so many times, and when the odds were against all my efforts,

God prevailed. Each year, I learn more about plants, food and preservation. My husband is now studying for hours to learn what plants need. Concerning food, we are doing what we can, hoping for the best, but planning for the worst.

The idea of emergency food being stockpiled is very important. On site, a person should have six months of food and water, in case of a natural disaster, war, terrorist attack, sickness, air poisoning, lack of rain, food shortage or crop failure, etc. Paper goods are really important for meals and more, including paper towels, paper plates, toilet paper and tissues. Canned goods last a really long time, and so does dried noodle soup. Try to buy items that expire in 3 to 4 years from the date you buy them. If you can remember to, you can rotate out the older food and keep eating it and replenishing with new food. We can't seem to remember to do that and in the case of a crisis, I have no issue eating food past the expiration date.

The design of the greenhouse was sketched out and then broken into sections that could be built individually. The wood lengths were optimized, so every scrap of wood was used. If small lengths were left over, then those were used for the angle supports in trusses or braces for the wind.

I built the greenhouse wall sections and roof trusses in my living room, and they have metal brackets for stability. They were manageable and easier to store under the roof on the back porch, until I was ready for assembly. We assembled on location, and added many more support braces for high winds. The size is 14 feet wide and seven feet deep. The walk-in door is just under 6 feet high. The roof peak is 8 feet tall. The header

beam has a shelf for storing grit, chicken feeders and waterers, and more! The budget was $350, but in the second year more wood was bought, along with some paint, and two windows. That was approximately $300. In the third year I got rid of the bad plastic that got brittle, and replaced it with something really great. I believe it was $140 for that.

In the second year, I added more roof support 1"x2"s so that the plastic will not gap or hang down with rain or ice on it. We get monsoon-style rain here sometimes, so this was an important change to make.

The roof and walls of the greenhouse are now a plastic that is specially reinforced 12ml and is really durable in the elements, as well as strong. The advertisements show that this plastic will suspend an F-150 truck! I believe it.

There are two windows that open and have screens. I should have four windows, and it is a goal for next year to buy and install those. They are now double in cost, thanks to inflation.

The workbench is so great, because

potting plants can be done, and special treatments can be made. The hydrogen peroxide and water mix for spraying on plants is easily made and bottled on the workbench.

Everything was protected with green paint after the build was done, except the treated lumber.

I store gallon bottles of water in the greenhouse for the chickens, as well as watering plants faster and easier. The greenhouse serves as a barn to a certain extent, as I keep pine shavings, feed, scratch, and straw in there as well, for the chickens.

Seeds are planted a month or two before outdoor planting is possible, so we are transplanting stronger plants when the frost is gone. I do have a

Chapter 11 - Food to Eat and for the Soul

heater that sits on the workbench, to run on low when it is cold at night.

Cedar chips are on the sloped floor over top of fabric weed block. This is clean, absorbent and keeps away bugs.

Garden planners are fun to use, but I now companion plant and just draw it out on a sheet of paper.

I try to bring in some plants to overwinter them. It is not always successful, as some winters are too cold, even with a heater running. I still had flowers in early December. One night at -11F and

it was over. It wasn't possible to heat for a week at really low temps outdoors, so I didn't try. The plants that wither and die do have seeds you can harvest in the spring.

When gardening, it is important to plan all crops out in advance. Research companion planting, as this will cut down on pests and reduce the need for insecticides. Most home-made pest repellents are not going to work very well. Nature works best, putting plants together that naturally protect each other.

The first greenhouse was a stand-up style. It was basically a failure, for our needs, because not much could be grown in there. It was convenient to stand and work, however, so flowers would be nice in this type of construction. If you are older, this is definitely nice, and you can have a couple of tomato plants and beans, etc.

I did repurpose the wood from the stand-up style greenhouse, and used it to make the compost bin.

The compost bin is really going to work over a period of time, and I got some nice dark dirt filled with worms and other goodies. I put fruit and vegetable scraps, dead leaves, old plants, straw and chicken coop poop in there. It is expensive to buy compost and you never really get good quality material like you can make at home.

Chapter 11 - Food to Eat and for the Soul

Eventually, we tilled up a huge area, to extend the small garden, and fenced it completely in. I had individual plots that got overrun with weeds and the soil is clay. It was hard to feed the plants when the soil was so compacted. I had to feed and till a lot. I was discouraged.

After a few years, I built the five raised garden beds, but filling them with dirt was difficult. I started with cardboard, straw, and sticks in alternating layers. I added soil and compost.

We did have to have a soil and compost mix delivered for the raised garden beds this year. Our soil is clay, so it is not great in the beds. The load was dumped in one area and then we had to shovel each bed full. That was hard work.

The compost bin yielded some nice dark compost this year, but not a huge amount. I need to be more faithful in filling the compost bin with everything that I can.

The wheelbarrow is an old one from my childhood that we used when I was a child, so one of my grandsons and I reconditioned it, because it is sentimental.

The whole garden, including the chicken coop, is fenced in with welded wire or chain link fence, with a gate to come in and out. That gate is wide enough for the wheelbarrow to fit through. This year, due to raccoons, I added another layer high of deer fence, so it is fenced six feet high, and we got the sonic mole

and raccoon repellers.

We tried the electric fence idea. The project was time-intensive and not worth the effort. It is hard cutting the weeds all around 150 feet of fence. For two years we did not need the electric fence. That may change due to the raccoons, but right now we are not using it. We have sensor LED lights at night. It helps to have a dog, too.

We had an upper area garden for corn, but that failed due to the weed growth and the distance from our home, so the materials were brought to the main house garden.

Using the chicken droppings, we have great fertilizer. Mixing a bucket of 10% dried droppings to a bucket of water and stirring for a couple of hours on and off, you get a nice liquid fertilizer. I put the thicker mixture in cat litter buckets, and the 25% diluted mixture in one-gallon jugs. Look on the web for each plant, but some plants can have this nitrogen once a week, and some only for the beginning of their growth. Either way, it is free and easy to make.

The raised beds are built from cedar pickets like you would use for a picket fence. They are the only cedar wood that is affordable, with a tight budget. It

cost $200 for the five raised beds. I made two beds deeper, using the cement blocks, because we had them extra from another project. The corners are strong because they are attached using 2x4s and exterior screws. The cardboard, sticks, straw, and compost are in layers in each box. I tried to keep wood chips on the paths between the boxes, so the rain doesn't make mud in the walkways. I put the chicken tea on the raised beds, and also worm castings. In the corn garden, lime is also spread over the area.

Learning about what grows around you on your land is important. Foraging is an

Chapter 11 - Food to Eat and for the Soul

important skill to learn. Do you have wild onions, berries, mushrooms, nuts, or other plants that are good to eat? What would be used for medicine? You can explore and find out! There are some good books out there with drawings and photos that show each plant, as well as have recipes for using the plants.

Consider food sources such as a fish pond or using aquaponics for growing. If you study some of the methods, it can be something beneficial to try.

We have sweet peppers, medium peppers and hot peppers in the garden

each year, so we enjoy making fajitas with all the fresh peppers. Cook the peppers and onions in a fair amount of oil and simmer on the stove. Pour all of that cooled mixture over the lean beef cut into strips and put in the fridge overnight. This marination makes the best fajita meat, and when ready, place all of the mixture on the grill! It will flare up due to the oil, so if you don't like handling that, you can separate the onion and pepper mixture out onto paper towels to get rid of some of the excess oil. Cook the meat by itself on the covered grill until blackened, and then add the peppers and onions on top of the meat for the last 5 to 10 minutes. Either way, it is delicious. Put the meat into flour tortillas with cheese and taco sauce or salsa, and enjoy!

Bonfires are nice to have with the family all around for the Fourth of July or any other holiday. We no longer use the original bonfire pit that was dug out and encircled with the sandstone rocks that are so beautiful. The sandstone here is pretty rosy pink with white stripes.

We now have a metal fire pit, with a grate and screen, so you can cook hot dogs and s'mores over that as well. It is safer, as there is a mesh over it, so embers will not be blown into the dry leaves. We do not have grass here, in the forest. On the ground we have sticks and dry leaves, only. We don't need a lawn mower, really, in most places.

In Kentucky, we are grilling outdoors year-round, and the smell of charcoal on a winter's day is wonderful. It makes the winter seem shorter somehow.

The first grill setup included a bench, but we didn't use it that much, so we used the materials for another project. We had a nice cast iron grill originally, which was about $120, but even though it got covered most of the time, it rusted out.

Eventually, we built an area that was bigger and we added a second grill. We just buy the cheap $15 grills and replace them when we need to.

It is a nice project to build a pizza oven for making pizzas, breads and many other dishes. That is the next project for us. We will study the ideas others have, and see what works for us. Like everything else, it costs money for cement and fire bricks.

I would love this outdoor cooking space to also have a meat processing area with a stainless steel counter for processing and cutting venison.

Think about ways of cooking food. It is important to have spices, oil and lard for cooking. Stainless pans are good.

The electric smoker is one of our favorite cooking areas for making large meals. The smoker has a water and apple juice area that is filled for flavor. We rub the baked potatoes in lard and then season with onion powder, salt and pepper, after microwaving them for a short time first. The pork loin, chicken thighs, pork roasts and baked beans are really excellent in the smoker! We do put a rub on the meat and let it marinate in the fridge overnight. The BBQ sauce is put on one hour before the meat is taken out of the smoker to eat. If you consider getting a smoker, get the biggest one you can afford, because it really only holds enough for 10 people, or for meat you could freeze for over the course of a week.

Smokers can be fueled with propane, wood, charcoal, wood pellets, or electric. There may be more choices out there. I would like to try a wood smoker, as I feel that would have the most robust flavor. Of course, we do add wood chips to the smoker while it is cooking, and we have mesquite, apple, cherry and hickory on hand to choose from.

We depend on God for spiritual and physical sustenance. We should thank God, aloud, for our food and ask Him to nutritionally bless it to our bodies. The spoken Word also has power to provide protection. Say grace; be thankful.

Chapter 12 – Explore the Forest

Deuteronomy 2:7 For the Lord thy God hath blessed thee in all the works of thy hand: he knoweth thy walking through this great wilderness: these forty years the Lord thy God hath been with thee; thou hast lacked nothing.

Every day, you can walk through your land and notice something new. You can watch wild animals, notice water running deeper in a creek during the spring, enjoy new migrating birds, see butterflies, and hear peepers peeping. The flocks of turkeys are impressive with their loud clattering! Sooner or later, we forget the old life and sounds. It seems as though this peace and nature was the only thing we ever knew.

> Spring brings the brilliant yellow and green of daffodils amongst the brown and gray left from winter. They are so hardy that if it snows on them, they will be fine – shining all the more brightly against white!

When the spring rains come, it can be torrential and the erosion can be significant. If you note what is flooding or eroding, you can make barriers of old logs and rocks, or dig ditches for water runoff. With nature you see the beauty and the power. If you work with nature, you will learn and understand as time goes by. Nature is something to admire and respect.

Summer is lush in the forest, so quiet and has an enclosed feeling. You can't see through the trees and all the bushes and vegetation mute any sounds from the outside world. It is so dense that it feels like a jungle at times.

Picking all of the blackberries and

raspberries is so fun and we all love to do it. We find new bushes each year.

We have spiders and snakes that need to be identified and avoided. Black widow and brown recluse are two spiders that live here and they are poisonous. We have poisonous snakes including timber rattlers, copperheads, northern cottonmouth, and western pygmies.

Of course, we deal with insects such as ticks. This is important to protect yourself against, as ticks carry diseases. Commercial insect repellent is necessary, as I have made many natural concoctions that were not effective. Not only were they ineffective, but the ingredients were expensive as well.

Many fun activities also include good exercise. Hiking, locating natural springs, and plant identification is enjoyable. My husband also started metal detecting and digging for treasures. So far, he has dug up a bit of

historical items, and after a lengthy full-sun dig one day, we located an old beer can. Sad face. Cleaning the trails and trimming berry bushes and wild roses can be challenging, but necessary. Early morning and late afternoon is cooler for these types of activities. Most activities on the homestead are good exercise.

Autumn days, we enjoy picking up branches blown down in storms, and we break those into smaller pieces for kindling for the wood stove. We keep that wood in a box under the porch roof and in a box under a tarp. It will be nice and dry for the next winter season. The fall season is great for getting ready for winter. The colors are usually golds and oranges, and the sunlight on the forest path is inviting. A gentle breeze and crispy leaves underfoot is a peaceful feeling of solitude.

We have a lot of quartz here laying on the ground exposed after a torrential downpour. It is pretty to collect and use in the garden or even in the pet cemetery. We have not yet found them, but our area has geodes also.

Winter really doesn't last that long here, in KY, but it can set records and be pretty intense at times. Some of the record-setting winters have had three feet more of snow, or had ice storms four months earlier in the year or been the coldest in 26 years! It is so pretty with snow on every branch, if just for a day or two. It is like fairyland and it is so quiet. We try to throw bread and corn to the deer, and feed our forest birds. We tend to get a lot of bluejays and cardinals.

During storms we have come to the conclusion it is best to stay home. We go out to get a few pieces of wood and admire the scenery. Some winters can be extreme with either deep snow or ice storms that last many days. The interstate highway was shut down for 19 hours one year, and the National Guard had to come in and help trapped motorists with gas, blankets, water and food. They even used Humvees to extract people out of the area, due to some people having medical emergencies.

We could not get to our home with our 4X4 truck at times, so we used the side-by-side to bring in groceries during some winters. These are difficult periods. We keep the tarp on the side-by-sde, to protect us from wind and to keep snow off the seat. In winter, we normally leave the truck or car away from our home, in a better location on our land, so we can go to town if there is ice or deep snow in our driveway.

There are wild grape vines, but even when we try to prune the smaller ones, we seldom see actual grapes. If we see some, they are really small. It will require more studying to figure out how to get the wild grapes to produce.

We have many type of moss growing, as well. It is really pretty.

Flowers are everywhere, and we are quite happy seeing all of the butterflies and turtles. The wildflowers are great for

Chapter 12 - Explore the Forest *Page 97*

the garden area for pollination, and we do have quite a few hummingbirds, as well.

Finding wood for garden borders is always nice. I like to find straight limbs that can be used for outlining planting areas.

Our driveway is steep, winding and has a deep drop-off into a gully in one area, so ice and snow can be intense. We don't want to flip over down the embankment. Each year, we see more erosion. Some years we see extreme ice or really deep snow.

Before we purchased the side-by-side, we had an especially bad winter and the 4x4 truck had to be left at the top of the steep driveway, and could not be driven to our home. We came back from getting groceries at night and we had to walk all the way in and up to the house. I carried bags of groceries, and my husband carried the giant bag of dog food on his shoulder. We went down in and around the winding driveway, then through the gully and way up to the steep incline to the top where our home is located. It was in the dark and in deep snow all the way to our cabin. After that experience, my husband bought the side-by-side UTV. After that, I made sure we never needed to go to a store in a storm, and we have kitty litter, water, food, pet food and everything we need.

In summer, before you sit in any lawn chair, you tip it forward to check for bees that might be building a nest or hive in the chair back. We usually spray insecticide to deter the bees from building their homes. This year my husband discovered that Permethrin spray will coat the decks and porches to deter bees from building nests or drilling holes in the wood. On a cold night, I usually use a putty knife and scrape the hornet and wasp bee hives off into a glass jar. The kids can take those to school to show classmates.

People around here enjoy finding mushrooms. If you study mushrooms, meet with cooperative extension or have a neighbor go with you, then you can learn which mushrooms are safe and which ones are poisonous. I have a book about mushrooms and how to identify them properly, as well as how to prepare them.

In fall, the colors are pretty, but much more muted than in NY or PA.

> **Enjoying nature's smells, sounds, wildlife, budding trees, blossoming flowers, birds, and fresh air are some things many people never get to do. It is healing and calming.**

We have unlimited ferns growing and they can be strategically planted as they are ornamental. If you wanted to sell them in pots, you could do that, as most stores charge

$19.99 each for them. Think about what you can use from nature, to make a little extra money.

The back deck overlooks the forest and deep valley where the deer come to eat. It is always pretty to see, no matter what season it is. In winter, the leaves are mostly gone, and we can see more clearly.

Chapter 13 – Discover the Calm

Philippians 4:7 And the peace of God, which passeth all understanding, shall keep your hearts and minds through Christ Jesus.

Living remotely or in a secluded place gives privacy and a quiet life. We study God's Word and we walk in peace, in nature. We are immersed in God's creation. We are apart from the chaotic and man-made noise of the world.

1 John 3:2-3 Beloved, now are we the sons of God, and it doth not yet appear what we shall be: but we know that, when he shall appear, we shall be like him; for we shall see him as he is. 3 And every man that hath this hope in him purifieth himself, even as he is pure.

Enjoying the forest escape is easy. There is so much to be thankful for and you can't ignore it, the moment you walk outside. In the dawn of a new day, it is stunning how blanketed and quiet it feels. It is damp but not cold in the mornings, and the fog is present many days. The deer enjoy this moment. Even the birds are quiet. Later in the day, in full sun working in the garden, time has no place. Butterflies and dragonflies land, then dart away. Birds are singing in the trees. I see little lizards and frogs. This is truly the life God blesses us with - if we accept it.

Garden problems can be solved, and plants grow lush. Picking peppers and tomatoes, and putting them in a little basket, is satisfying.

I enjoy feeding the chickens a little scratch and talking to each one, being sure to praise the roosters, too. Gathering eggs in the evening is wonderful. I always thank the girls for such good work! They do listen.

Making dinner with fresh vegetables is so important, and tasty of course. Getting the work done in the course of the day is all that matters; there is no real hurry to do most things at a particular time.

People always ask if we get lonely and the answer is not one little bit. We are always busy, so there is no time to sit and think about being alone in the forest. We text and email and conference call like everyone else, but on our terms. That is certainly enough. We go shopping and out on discovery drives around the area. The point is we choose to live secluded, but we can interact in society on our terms. It is a choice to do that, or not. When we return home it is a relief, to be totally honest.

> *1 Peter 3:15-17*
> *But sanctify the Lord God in your hearts: and be ready always to give an answer to every man that asketh you a reason of the hope that is in you with meekness and fear: 16 Having a good conscience; that, whereas they speak evil of you, as of evildoers, they may be ashamed that falsely accuse your good conversation in Christ. 17 For it is better, if the will of God be so, that ye suffer for well doing, than for evil doing.*

Some people criticize a choice to withdraw from society. They want everyone to have stress, struggle, and be subject to a bad environment. If they can't or won't make good life choices, they want everyone to suffer along with them. Misery loves company. They may persecute us because we are different, we won't submit, or just because they are jealous. A person has to want this lifestyle change with all of their heart and be willing to do the hard work.

The reward for breaking free from the world's stronghold is that you feel calm. You feel peace with God. You put Him in the number one position in life, but the rest of the world will not understand this decision because they love the world more than they love God. They reinforce each other's decisions to ignore and reject God. You can have a complete withdrawal from society, or you can keep working. Even if you continue working at your full-time or part-time job, you will have your safe place to return to each night.

So, what will other people say, if we take the chosen path to a forest escape? It isn't like it happens to us by accident. We make a deliberate choice to change our lives. Family will probably understand us, and friends will stand by us. They might be curious about how it all works out, or even admire us. Of course, it isn't really about us: it is about our love for God and obeying His will for our lives. It is about taking a stand against evil.

Some psychologists commenting in online articles deride people for withdrawing from society to find a location of freedom, peace and quiet. They accuse people of being shy, people who avoid conflict or difficulty, or those who are antisocial. I would argue that some psychologists simply study the behavior of others and are they, themselves, doing nothing risky, requiring hard work, or making changes for logical reasons. The professionals talk and analyze, but we dream and work to accomplish our goals. We have the strength of character to find the approval of society unnecessary. The point is that we may be profiled for making a lifestyle change.

Some professionals state that anyone who wants to find a forest escape so to speak is suffering from anxiety, has aggressive tendencies, is unwilling to work for what they want, and are unable to find pleasure in experiences that others find enjoyable. If we act to avoid what causes us anxiety it should be considered as smart, rather than taking antianxiety drugs like approximately 50% of the people in the workforce do just to cope with stress. We are motivated, not aggressive, and we work hard to make a lifestyle change. We find pleasure in an environment of peace rather than chaos.

Another observation by some psychologists is that we are rejected by our peers, or we are loners who don't want to interact with people. We are not rejected, but we reject the ways of the world that embrace evil. We interact with people, but we choose which kinds of people we hang out with. Our relationships are deeper and loyal, and we learn from each other with open minds. There are people who are leaders and those who are followers. Most people with very different perspectives on life are the types of people who change the world.

If we do not submit to the control of society, and we choose freedom and nature, we could be considered by psychologists as having issues. That is actually quite laughable. When society becomes unacceptable and full of deviant behavior, we are told to be tolerant. Nobody has the right to tell us that we need to live saturated in a world of evil. It has become a hostile environment where children are constantly bombarded with a world of violence, persecution, impossible comparatives, and unattainable objectives that yield no happiness. How many influencers have had money, beauty, and material things, as well as amazing popularity, and yet they commit suicide? It is a shallow life and God is not present in modern society. We can choose an alternative life in peace, in nature, and loving our Father in Heaven.

We need to take a stand or we will fall for anything. The time is now to say "no more" to what we find troublesome. We will forge our way, realize our dreams and triumphantly live free.

We will educate our children and grandchildren in a way that teaches the Bible, math, science, reading, writing, language, music, art, practical life skills, survival techniques, and so much more. We will not teach the various evil concepts that are being embraced and propagated by those with no mental fortitude to fight back.

Evil prevails when good men do nothing.

Those who criticize our choices may try to label us as damaged goods. If the opposition can't understand us, or make us submit, then they will try to profile us as having issues. We will stand firm and prove that we excel in honorable ways, and we will not submit to the ways of the world that are contrary to our beliefs.

We will be the shining light on the hill and when the end time chaos comes, we will be strong and share the Gospel with others. We will help Christians have the strength to start on their chosen path, and to listen to the small still voice of the Holy Spirit. The peace comes from within and we can be calm in all situations. Don't apologize for wanting to live in a way that honors God.

2 Timothy 2:1-4 Thou therefore, my son, be strong in the grace that is in Christ Jesus. 2 And the things that thou hast heard of me among many witnesses, the same commit thou to faithful men, who shall be able to teach others also. 3 Thou therefore endure hardness, as a good soldier of Jesus Christ. 4 No man that warreth entangleth himself with the affairs of this life; that he may please him who hath chosen him to be a soldier.

Chapter 13 - Discover the Calm

Chapter 14 – Warmth on a Cold Night

Philippians 4:19 But my God shall supply all your need according to his riches in glory by Christ Jesus.

No matter where you live, having a heat source and a backup are important. Cooking is also possible with certain kinds of wood stoves.

If you have electric in your little cabin in the woods, you will need a generator for the times when there is an electricity outage. The outages happen frequently for thousands of people in many areas, and some of those outages can range from hours to days or weeks.

Other choices include wood, geothermal, coal, pellet, fuel oil, and propane. Do your research to see what you want. Also, everyone needs a backup. We have electric baseboard, electric space heaters, a generator, a wood stove, a propane furnace and a portable propane heater.

The wood stove keeps us warm and in an electric outage allows us to have hot water in the teapot. We could cook in the cast iron pan on top of the stove, if we

needed to. We use a propane torch, junk mail paper to start the fire, and we have creosote cleaner for the chimney pipe to ensure that it stays clean.

With the chainsaws, we cut wood from trees that have been cut down or fallen in the forest. Some of it is a year old and some of it is three years old.

I gather kindling from the forest floor, using a waxed canvas wood sling that allows me to carry a lot at once. We save the bark that comes from splitting the wood on the wood splitter. Extra chains, oil and gas are important to have in the storage shed.

The cut wood is unloaded from the side-by-side or truck, and is split in the wood splitter. The wood is stacked between some big trees, on pallets and then eventually stored on the back deck under the roof, and there is emergency wood in the generator overhang area. The idea is to keep the wind blowing through it, to dry it, so it burns nicely in the wood stove. Wet wood barely heats and gunks up your chimney pipe with creosote.

The wood stove needed wall protection and we had to do a lot of research to find something that would work properly and be safe with high temperatures. We chose a stone panel. The stove has a back heat shield, which is extra safe. The wood stove sits on an elevated platform with ceramic tiles on top. The stone and tiles are all grouted.

The warmth on a cold night is so pleasant

and the fire in the wood stove is something you can watch for hours.

I have a little red stainless teapot that will boil water on top of the wood stove, to make tea, and to generate humidity. It would be possible to cook a meal on top of this stove, using a cast iron pan. We could easily fry bacon and cook eggs, or heat a pan of soup.

It is really wonderful to use a wood stove, but of course it is hard work to cut, split and carry firewood. One log per hour, with the air flow shut in, maintains a pretty high temperature in the house and we have about a 16-foot ceiling in the living room/dining room area. The wood stove is very efficient.

There are multiple ways to start a fire. You can use a propane torch, fire starter sticks, matches and paper, cotton on petroleum jelly, or a lighter.

When the wind blows and it rains torrentially, then turns to sleet, and coats everything with ice in ever-dropping temperatures, we sit in the living room enjoying the dancing flames of the fire in the wood stove. The warmth is wonderful and the ambiance in the room is cozy. All the work of hauling in firewood into wood racks and crates is worth it.

The cats love watching the flames, and sleep near the wood stove to soak up the heat. The dog watches the fire, too. All is peaceful and quiet.

Hard work, with your hands, is tiring but satisfying. It brings about an appreciation for simple things. This aspect of life is missing in many jobs, as many jobs are mostly mental and not physical. Homesteading is both. Mentally it is challenging and physically it can be exhausting. We always have to think about working smarter instead of harder, so it is enjoyable.

I'm happy to avoid hurting my back, by using equipment and tools. We put wood in the back of the side-by-side to get it closer to the house, so we can bring it inside. Then, we carry loads of wood into the house crates and small wood rack, as well as through the house to the large back deck wood rack. We can use the wood sling, the dolly or just carry wood in our arms. It is important to exercise sensibly. We do sort the wood into kindling, starter slabs, fast-burning wood and long-burning wood.

When you choose a wood stove, get more stove than you need. We have a 1,200 sq. ft. cabin with an open ceiling in the living room/dining room area, and a loft upstairs. That means heat rises but also requires more heat for the lower floor. Our wood stove is rated for 2,500 sq. ft. and uses wood logs to heat. We bought the fan for it, but never use it. It can have an air intake in the back, but we didn't install it.

The wood stove has the glass airwash technology to keep the door glass clean. It is better than most, but still gets blackened if logs get near the glass. If you need to clean the glass of your stove, simply use a paper towel with a little of the ashes and a bit of water to wash the cold glass. Then, use clear water to rinse it and dry it. The door glass will look like brand new when you are done.

Ashes get cleaned out every three or four days and go into the garden.

Your chimney determines where your stove will be placed in the cabin or home. We chose the corner location and the fire can be seen by people on both couches in the living room.

We taped off the floor with painter tape, so we could envision the location and size. The hearth platform takes up more floor space than you would imagine.

The wood stove research is vital for fire code, for insurance purposes, and for safety in general. Our home insurance did not increase, so we feel quite lucky about that.

The wall protection makes sure that a fire won't start in the area of the wood stove. It requires a particular R value. We used stone tiles on the hearth and part of the wall. A decorative tile was used above that area and all was grouted. Unfortunately, we lost the internet connection box and two electrical outlets in building this wall protection area.

The platform for the hearth needs to have symmetrical 2"x4" construction with studs every 10" or so. Design the studs on paper, so you envision the tiles having support and there will be no gaps that cause cracking. Extra support goes where the stove will be located. It needs to be really strong, as the stove itself weighs an incredible amount. Our hearth is a 4-inch step up. We keep the fireplace tools on the hearth, as well as the covered ash bucket.

The chimney is complicated. The draft is particular and the chimney has to go above the roof a bit, as well as be securely attached to the house. Study the stove specs and the local regulations. Ask someone from your fire department, if you need extra advice. The chimney goes through the wall with a special kit that goes outdoors, has a cleanout fitting at that juncture, and then goes straight up to the cap on top. There is a kit to attach the chimney to the roof

and one to attach it to the side of the house. The cap on the top should have some type of grid to keep birds out.

When you are all done, it is a great feeling, and whatever room you put a wood stove in has changed considerably. You can feel confident that it was built properly, inspected and is safe. It is important not to overload the wood stove, to keep the chimney free of creosote, and to burn dry wood. Remember, the stove always has to be used in a safe manner. You can buy a wood log moisture meter for around $50 and it will help you burn only dry wood.

A smaller wood solution could be done yourself for $1,000 possibly, but our type of setup was $5,000 installed.

If you live in the forest, you will always be warm, because the wood is plentiful.

Chapter 15 – Hunting and Security

Psalms 91:4-5 He shall cover thee with his feathers, and under his wings shalt thou trust: his truth shall be thy shield and buckler. Thou shalt not be afraid for the terror by night; nor for the arrow that flieth by day;

Living remotely, partially off-grid or of-the-grid could require the hunting, raising, or trapping of animals. You will also be monitoring your premises, as well as protecting your family, animals, flocks, home, land, and outbuildings.

Hunting for food means that you will have venison to eat from killing a deer, or maybe turkey, squirrel or rabbit as food to grill over a fire. If you are lucky, you will have wild boar, ducks, pheasant or quail on your land. It is possible to have a nice variety of meat for food.

You could hunt with a bow or a gun, or by trapping. You would choose a particular gun for a particular task. Maybe a rifle for the deer, and a shotgun for the turkey. It means you will need ammunition, and gun cleaning kits and the know-how to use each firearm safely, and to keep them in good condition. It is important to practice regularly and to understand and practice firearm safety. If you have a bow, you will need to practice often to develop accuracy, and have the proper accessories, as well as different types of arrows. If you are trapping, you will need to study how to set the traps in areas where people do not walk, where to place them in the forest for particular wild game, and how to use traps safely, as well as to check them often.

In hunting with a rifle or shotgun, you will need to learn the best shot placements, to field dress an animal, and to prepare the meat for eating or preservation. Study posters with the shot placements, so you understand the anatomy of the animal you are hunting. Not only do you miss out on the meat, but nobody wants an animal to be wounded and then suffering in the forest. Field dressing is processing the carcass enough to get it to your location to later cut up the meat for steaks, roasts, stews, and more.

Consider how you will preserve the meat. If you freeze the meat, it will be long-term storage. If you make jerky, it will be dehydrated. Remember to keep the fat and cook it down, as it can be used in making pemmican and other long-term storage foods. Indians made pemmican from dry meat and animal fat and it could last for 6 months to 5 years, depending on the ingredients. There are many wonderful recipes on the internet for meats from wild game. Usually, onion and garlic are good to use with these meats. Imagine having a nice venison stew on a cold winter's night. The idea of cooking a meal from meat that you have hunted and processed is definitely a primal basic survival skill.

Carcass disposal needs to be done carefully, placed in your woods, far from your home and down wind. It will attract predators, so this is an important consideration.

The Fish and Wildlife Department produces a brochure or flyer with information, or you can go to the web site for the laws and hunting seasons each year.

The cuts of meat are different for each animal, but we can look at the deer for an example. Venison is the meat from the deer, and you can have roasts, steaks and so much more. The meat tends to be a little more dry than other types of meats, so some people mix ground venison with ground pork. If you don't like the gamey taste of

DEER - CUTS OF MEAT

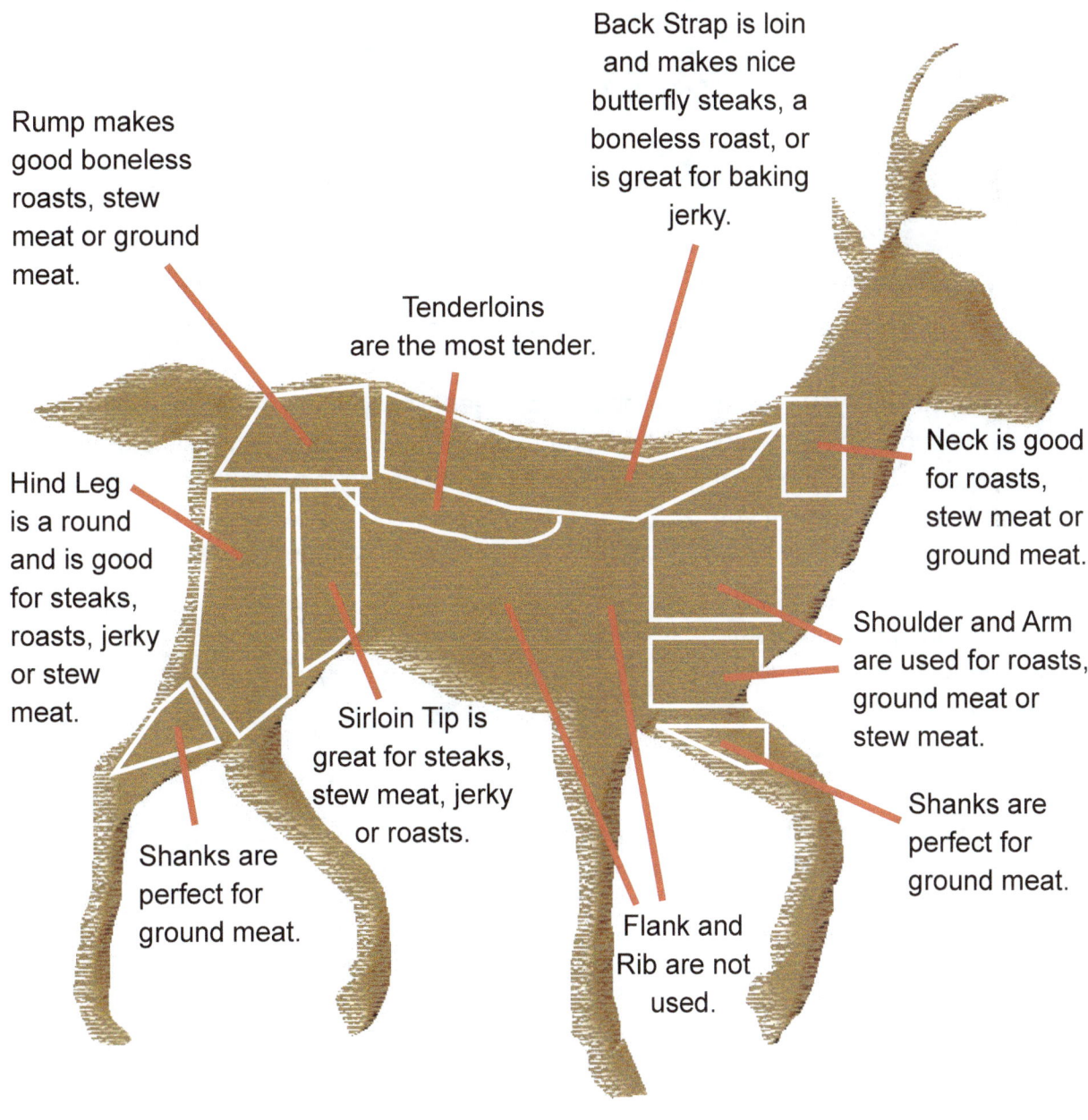

Rump makes good boneless roasts, stew meat or ground meat.

Back Strap is loin and makes nice butterfly steaks, a boneless roast, or is great for baking jerky.

Tenderloins are the most tender.

Neck is good for roasts, stew meat or ground meat.

Hind Leg is a round and is good for steaks, roasts, jerky or stew meat.

Shoulder and Arm are used for roasts, ground meat or stew meat.

Sirloin Tip is great for steaks, stew meat, jerky or roasts.

Shanks are perfect for ground meat.

Shanks are perfect for ground meat.

Flank and Rib are not used.

venison, you can soak the meat in milk, salt water, or a vinegar/water solution, and it removes that particular gamey taste. Cooking venison with onion or garlic is tasty.

Predators will stalk your chickens, rabbits and sheep. Many times this type of animal, such as a coyote, fox or raccoon will frequent your land. This means repelling, fencing out, or legally eliminating the threat. Notify the authorities, so they can keep track of animals that are around. If you have predators or animals that are pests, you may choose to trap them, and relocate them to another property. If large predatory animals come into a domestic area, it could be dangerous for pets, herds, flocks and people. Mountain lions have been known to attack a horse's foal. You may need the help of a game warden to assist you in getting rid of an unwanted bear, coyote, or mountain lion.

Feral cats live in the forest

many times because irresponsible and cruel people abandon their animals, and particularly cats are found in the forest. Many times these cats are also pregnant. The cats are cold and have trouble finding food or water.

We had a coyote out in the daylight walking in our home area, next to the storage building. We hope he moves along, but I have found that a gunshot into the scrub brush will scare coyotes away for the rest of the season, if need be.

Animals are not the only threat to people living in secluded areas. Criminals love to operate in privacy and may decide your area is great for drug trafficking or some other activity. Some people target cabins in the woods, wanting to steal guns or food. Home invasions happen. Some criminals use your forest to operate an illegal still for making moonshine, or build a small shack to cook methamphetamine. Maybe the bad guys grow marijuana on your property and you don't even see it. If you have a forest escape, you will need to patrol the roads and woods on your land to make sure nobody is doing anything illegal on it. The good thing is most police will fly over low in helicopters and look from time to time.

> We're not guaranteed safety in the city, nor in the countryside, but remember God is watching over us. Prayer daily works.

As long as there is functioning electricity and internet, a good home security system is vital, and a camera system to monitor the activity around your home and outbuildings is going to give you peace of mind. It is hard to find a "Made in the USA" system that is affordable. The screenshot here is a product that is made in America. An 8-camera security system is available for around $500. Make sure your video is being backed up in the cloud if you trust it, or remotely somewhere on a server, in case the thieves steal the security camera hard drive. Most systems are able to be accessed by an app, so you can check on your home if you are away from the area. The trail cams help you know what animals are in the area, and if people are going through your property. A good trail cam with good resolution images is about $80. A special chip reader can plug in your cell, so you can review and replace the SD card while you are at the trail cam site. There are many ways of attaching the cam to a tree, building or fence post, etc. You may want to lock it on with a chain and padlock.

Fences, signs, cameras, gates and chains keep equipment, roads, buildings and land safer. Invest in heavier and stronger items, as cheaper chains or locks can easily be cut. Cheap signs get destroyed by the weather. Mounting signs on wood and screwing the wood into the tree works best. Otherwise, the plastic signs just disintegrate or the squirrels nibble all four corners, and the sign shreds, falling onto the ground.

How you decide to protect your home, family, and animals is up to you and it should be in compliance with the law. It is important to know the laws in your state, and federal regulations as well.

Chapter 16 – Preserving

Luke 12:22 And he said unto his disciples, Therefore I say unto you, Take no thought for your life, what ye shall eat; neither for the body, what ye shall put on.

Growing a garden, hunting, raising a flock or herd to provide food, and preserving food for winter months could be easy for you, or it could prove to be difficult. Don't worry, it will be easier each year. You will discover new preservation methods each year. A friend or neighbor can help you get started.

Preservation normally means that the processed food will need to avoid humidity, air and sunlight after being preserved.

Dehydration is interesting, no matter the method that you use to do it. You can buy a dehydrator and use the electric source to process fruits over 14 hours, or to make beef or venison jerky over 4 to 6 hours. Some recipes use salt, soy sauce or some use nitrate for a preservative. Look for trusted recipes online or in cookbooks. Marination of the meat prior to the dehydration process really helps in making flavorful jerky. Dehydrated food can easily be put in zipper bags, or vacuum sealed in plastic bags. Study the historical methods of salt preservation for ham, etc.

Canning food is great because you can have fresh tomato

sauce on your spaghetti in the middle of winter, or apple pie simply by pouring the canned apples into a pie crust! The peace of mind of seeing rows of jars of food for the cold season is really important. Following the science of canning properly is vital. We use the Ball canning jars and their web site for proper recipes to make sure the food was correctly processed.

We have water bath canning equipment, but with shortages, it is advisable to buy what you need well before the season starts for preserving food. Citric acid, canning jars, canning jar lids, and thickener for fruits were previously in short supply. One year, we could not find quart size glass jars anywhere. I do prefer the pint jars for many things, as it is enough for a meal for two people. The quart jar may have too much and it is fine if you have the fridge. If you don't, then it could be a concern to keep the food from spoiling once opened.

We have made apple butter, pickles, apple pie filling, tomatoes, jams and jellies, and more! It is fun and the kids really love all of these special canned foods. I especially love making spaghetti in the winter, using the jars of tomatoes. The spaghetti sauce tastes better, too, compared to store-bought sauce.

The pressure canner is also a nice piece of equipment for the kitchen. It is for preserving low-acid foods such as meat, seafood, poultry, vegetables, soups, and more.

Many people specialize in fermenting as a way of preservation. Learning about that could be fun. I have not tried it.

During wars, hard tack was made. It is basically a flat biscuit with holes in it and made of flour, water and salt. It lasts a really long time. Find recipes to make an emergency food that historically was eaten by sailors and soldiers!

Peppers are great, because you can hang them to dry, refrigerate and freeze them.

American Indians made pemmican. This is primarily made of dry meat and animal fat, and is sometimes made with berries and honey. The longest lasting pemmican is with meat and fat only. Dried meat and rendered fat when properly preserved will last a really long time. Find recipes and make printed copies for your library. Imagine being snowbound or unable to leave your forest escape. This emergency food would come in handy!

Save your non-GMO vegetables' seeds, dry them and store them for the next planting season.

Smoking food is really wonderful and there are many methods. Charcoal smokers, electric smokers and wood smoke houses are some choices that you could implement in your homestead. The smell is heavenly, and the foods taste so good.

Freezing food is easy, and you can freeze individual items and cook only what you need. We always have garden peppers and beans through the winter. We freeze berries and tomatoes, too. It is important to have a good stock of frozen food for times you are not able to get to the store. We don't have to leave the house in winter snow and ice, tornado, or severe thunderstorms. We are working on stocking up items in bulk, to save money. If you only buy meat and vegetables that are on sale, then you will save so much money in the future, as inflation continues to rise.

Raising chickens to produce eggs is great because many people say that with refrigeration eggs with their bloom intact can last six month in the best-case scenario or possibly a month or more on the counter without refrigeration. Do your research to decide what experts say about the longevity of farm-fresh eggs.

God provides. As Christians, we never have to worry. A good neighbor might check in on us also, and bring a gift of food. That is how it used to be. Good people, good churches and good pastors used to visit and bring a little something to eat, to people less fortunate. They would meet needs. It is needed now, more than ever. Let's plan to do this! I recently gave a box of about 60 eggs to a lady to share with neighbors.

Canned apple pie filling is delicious and makes a nice dessert in the winter!

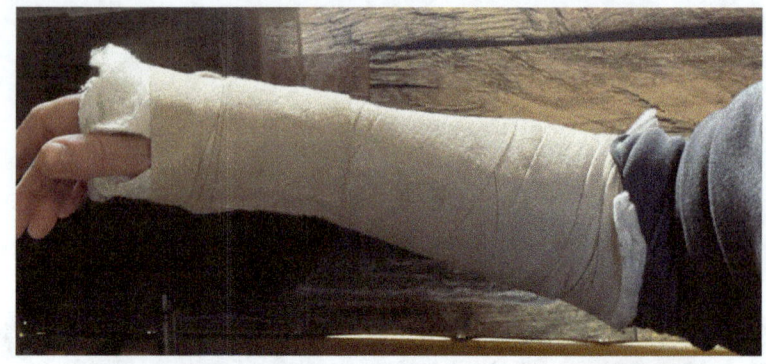

The urgent care solution was fiberglass for my broken wrist.

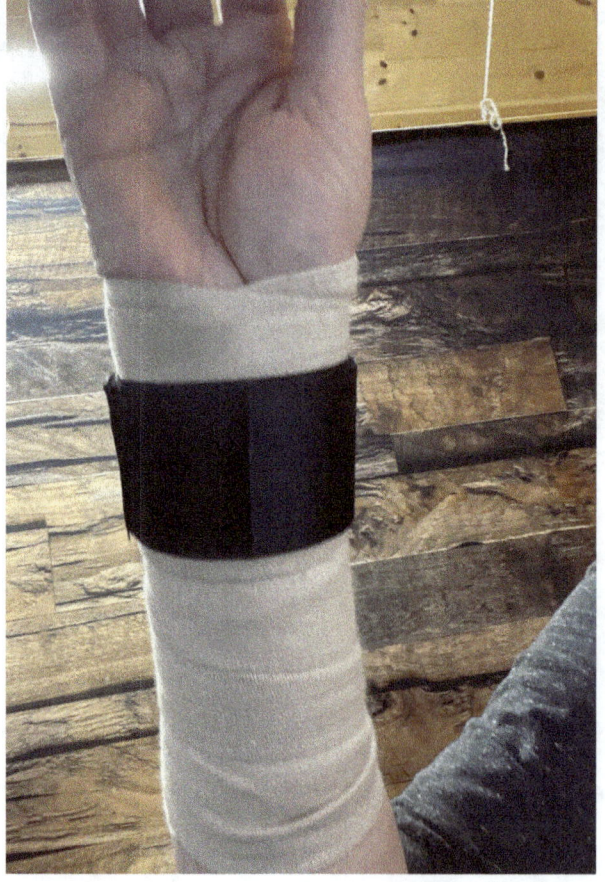

The fiberglass cut into my elbow and hand, as well as prohibited using a computer mouse, so I cut it off and replaced it with a sports wrap and industrial Velcro.

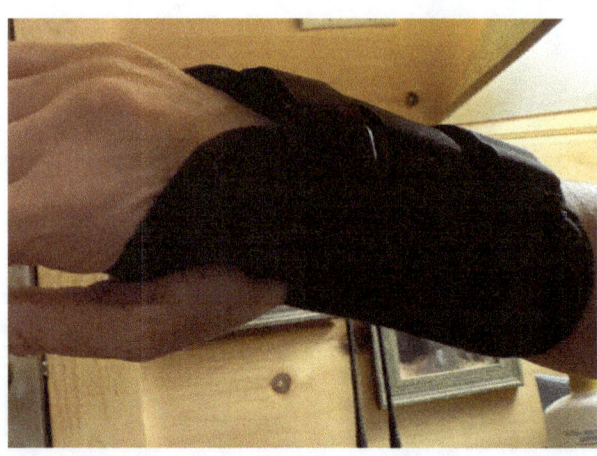

The orthopedic doctor gave me a proper wrist brace, with my promise not to lift heavy objects for six weeks.

Chapter 17 – Medical / Emergencies

Nahum 1:7 The Lord is good, a strong hold in the day of trouble; and he knoweth them that trust in him.

It is important to think about emergencies that might need to be handled, and injuries or sicknesses that you, your loved ones, or neighbors could suffer from. If you research and print out topics for basic first aid, and buy books about natural medicines, you could feel some confidence in handling most situations. Emergencies could include construction accidents, cutting or burning yourself cooking, injuries from hail, falling on the ice, breaking a bone, spider or snake bites, or stepping on a rusty nail. Illnesses could include the flu, food poisoning, the common cold, pneumonia, allergies, and poison ivy.

I have a book for foraging and those plants that are identified also have medical applications and recipes included. I have not tried making the medicines. If you get burned, you probably know that aloe is good to put on the skin. There is even a kind that is drinkable to use internally for ailments. I have made the insect repellents from natural extracts. I bought the ingredients online and made the mixtures and put them in spray bottles. They would work to a certain level if you had nothing available at the store to buy.

What should we have on hand? Some medicines can be stockpiled. It is useful to have iodine, isopropyl alcohol, ammonia, witch hazel, allergy medicines, vinegar, and peroxide in your emergency medicine cupboard. Bandage, tape, a sling, butterfly stitches, and adhesive bandages are important. Asking the doctor for extra prescriptions to have on hand could also be useful. A suture kit is also useful, if you need to clean a wound and stitch it up. Wrist, knee and ankle braces are useful. Many preppers talk about veterinary medicines such as amoxicillin and cephalexin to have on hand, as well, and you have to decide if that is an option for you. You can buy personal size cans of oxygen online, for breathing issues. An oxygenation meter is good to see the oxygen level in your blood. Insulin test kits, blood pressure cuffs and a stethoscope are good to have. Each family has different needs.

I encourage you to buy a big bottle of tea tree oil that is authentic and pure, because it has wonderful properties, and is antifungal, antiviral, antiseptic and antibacterial.

Natural medicine from herbs and plants can be made if you study from trusted sources. A good library of information is helpful and a good first aid kit is vital.

Knowledge is the most important tool. A good range of medical books in your library, containing how to handle any medical issue, is a wonderful resource to have on hand.

In terms of medical issues in the last 12 years, we have not had any major problems. At our location, we have had minor burns, shocks, lacerations, abrasions, Covid, extreme allergic responses, falls with bruises, heat exhaustion, spider bites, bee stings and tick bites. Only a couple of incidents required going to the doctor or hospital. The wrist incident was at a public place.

Emergencies can include fires or floods. It is important to have a good fire extinguisher, and a sump pump if you are prone to having water in your lower elevation living space. With the wood stove, there is a log for immediately putting out the fire in the chimney, so that is also something good to have on hand.

A good bugout bag is important, too, as well as an emergency bag in your car or truck, or on your ATV, or in your UTV, as the law allows. Basics like water, flashlight, lighter, change of clothes, emergency poncho and blanket, compass, jacket, hat, gloves, food, walkie-talkie, tarp, knife and weapon of your choice, radio, first aid kit, insect repellent, cash, etc. are great to have in a bag for emergencies.

The emergency stockpile of water, food, animal food, ammunition, heat and fuel is important. You need lighting of some type, too. Candles should be in special holders. The propane lantern is a good choice. The small propane space heater is great in winter.

You can find many documents and checklists for handling emergencies of all types on the internet from trusted sources. A copy of each type of emergency response is important to have on hand.

If you need to leave in a hurry, your important papers should be accessible, put in a waterproof bag, and able to be quickly taken with you if you have to leave your location, including birth certificate, insurances, deed, licenses, etc. Don't forget proper boots, medicines, a jacket, cash and credit cards, and a change of clothing.

If there is a national or regional emergency, such as a terrorist attack, tornado, hurricane, ice storm, biological attack, nuclear emergency, EMP, or chemical spill, there should be a plan that will help you survive and function after that event. A safe room, storm shelter or bunker is something to consider building one day. You would want to have all your supplies on hand, so you do not need to leave your home in times of stress.

So, we think about everyday issues like injuries, or even severe storms that cause damage and seem quite important, but there are other crises that are more extreme, and affect our state or our nation as a whole. There are natural disasters and there are terrorist attacks. This is a completely different level of crisis.

Natural disasters could include earthquakes, mudslides, solar flares, flooding or torrential rain, tornadoes and straight-line winds, hurricanes, snow and ice, no power, no communication and no heat, or some other consequence. This type of situation requires the ability to survive in difficult conditions, without normal conveniences. It means that you have to consider these things and have emergency supplies and a plan.

Terrorist attacks or even some types of accidents can include chaos, demonstrations, chemical, biological, radiological, electromagnetic pulse (EMP), nuclear, financial collapse, supply failures and more. These types of situations can include poisoned air, water or land. Attacks happen where there are soft targets with lots of people gathered and not really paying attention or being vigilant. Hard targets have security. High-value targets are regarded by the enemy as necessary objectives. If there is an attack, you have to have thought this through and have a plan, as well as supplies to survive.

> **When you are building your home or outbuilding of any kind, it is the perfect time to consider building safe spaces in the home and having safe retreat places in the forest.**

You need to be safe and secure, and the idea of shelter in place is usually the best scenario, but if you need to bug out, then remember the bugout bag should be ready to go at all times. If you buy the military survival manual online, it will help you. Prepare for impending crises by having clean dishes, clean clothes and towel, and doors locked and loose items fastened. Try not to go outdoors during bad weather, social unrest or crises.

The most important part of handling an emergency is that you have thought about it in advance, and that you can remain calm. You can proactively plan for any of this, and methodically respond to the situation in the appropriate way.

If there is social unrest, a terrorist attack, or an invasion of our country, we need to be able to hear the news, work together with neighbors, and defend our homes, neighborhoods and state. Local militias that are Constitutional are important. We have to be careful that we are not dealing with groups that are causing chaos. We need an orderly response and a lawful response, unless we are locally at war. If there is a war situation, then survival is number one. There are Christian militias that have leaders operating in ranks, practice scenarios, and can be helpful. Many members have previous law enforcement or military service, and are trustworthy.

Some administrative government officials and politicians dislike the idea of the citizen militia, but it is our right and duty to have one. It is becoming more and more unpopular with the government for citizens to own guns, which is also our right and duty. These topics are important because this is how we control the government and keep it from becoming more oppressive and tyrannical. The government is here to serve us, and it must adhere to The Constitution of the United States of America. Never does it say we lose our rights, if there is a crisis. If we allow liberty to be taken away, we may never get it back. False Flag events could then change our country forever and take away our freedom, in the name of fear, safety or security. Study the Constitution, so you know your rights. We must continue to fight to be free. Donate to good groups, patronize good companies, sign petitions, volunteer for good causes, demonstrate legally, and vote for good politicians with good hearts. Christians should not be timid, nor blind.

If you choose to be a part of social media, read the main stream news, and listen to politicians, test these sources for truth. Make sure it isn't a virtual reality. Corroborate your information from diverse sources. They, as in any group, can tell you anything - it doesn't make it true. Look around you and see what is real. Actively live life and test what is real, using your senses, your sensibilities, you spiritual eyes and your spiritual ears. With technology, they can create a pretend world, and it is amazing how many people are deceived. There is a saying that if you tell the same lie enough times, not only will people believe it, you, yourself, will come to believe it. Be ready for the emergencies, the crises and the deception. Watch and pray, for God is in charge.

Chapter 18 – Love Thy Neighbour

Matthew 22:37-39 Jesus said unto him, Thou shalt love the Lord thy God with all thy heart, and with all thy soul, and with all thy mind. This is the first and great commandment. And the second is like unto it, Thou shalt love thy neighbour as thyself.

We are commanded to love our neighbors by Jesus. We naturally care about neighbors, but when times are tough, do we really love them? That means sharing what you have, encouraging them and helping them. Love is work. Neighbors can cause issues, be difficult and have personal problems. We are also not perfect people, in the opinion of our neighbors. But, if we follow our Lord's commandment, none of that negativity matters. We have agape love, through the grace of God.

> Sharing, trading, bartering, selling, caring, encouraging, protecting and more, is so important.

If you have neighbors living near your forest escape, you will plan to be there for each other when life is difficult. If it is snowing and one of you is stuck or slips into a ditch, then you will help each other. When

your garden yields good vegetables you will share, and so will they. Maybe they have honey bees and make honey. Maybe you preserve apple pie filling. A trade is certainly a wonderful thing! Maybe one of you is sick and the other will help around the house with chores. If someone needs a warmer jacket and you have an extra one, you can give a neighbor that jacket. Maybe you have an expensive tool you could lend

to the neighbor so he could complete a project faster and easier. It is about compassion. You have heard the expression "What would Jesus do?", so this can be your mindset.

When we were building our forest escape, the one and only neighbor on our road at the time brought food to us almost daily, as we went in and out of our driveway. It is not something any of us will ever forget. It was God's love and the theme of love thy neighbour from the Bible in action. They saw us struggling and they made life simpler by giving us cooked items, garden items and so much more! It seemed like this continual compassion lasted almost a year! Today, we give them chicken eggs

each week, trying to repay them for their acts of kindness. They witnessed our true pioneer experience from clearing the land, to building in the middle of the forest, to establishing a road in the deep mud, to losing a beloved pet, to struggling without enough money to complete many important projects.

People in the neighborhood within a few miles all need things. You might be able to get to know people enough to ask for favors, and they might ask you as well.

If you need to raise money, you might be able to sell items to neighbors, too, if you have the skills to make things. If you know how to repair vehicles, ATVs, equipment or appliances, you might be able to get $20 here or there.

You could sell items on the internet, also, so you could make some extra money. You would need to be able to ship packages weekly.

Even a little extra money coming in from multiple sources is a good thing. Plan your shipping, shopping and fuel fill-ups on the same day to save on gasoline. Don't forget to ask the neighbor if they need anything, when you go.

Most of all, if things get out of hand and there is no electricity or no money or no food, then you would be there for each other. If thieves come or if security is needed, you would be there one for the other. We can trade items that are needed. It is smart to have on hand things that other people might need.

> What will be of value if the financial system fails? A lot of people with experience in war-torn countries will tell you lighters, batteries, ammunition, bottled water, medicines, blankets, etc., are all sought-after items. Of course food is also good. It is important to check on neighbors, to be sure they are okay, healthy, and not in need of something. Think of the neighbor as an extended family.

It might be hard to communicate with a neighbor if the phone service or electricity is not working. If you have an aerosol boat siren, alarms, or maybe clicking your vehicle FOB alarm could alert your neighbor that you need help. Of course, a gunshot or two might also get your neighbor's attention. We always check on each other, if there is a strange sound or a vehicle around that is not usual. If we all have generators and CB radios or mobile CBs, we can communicate on the hour as part of a planned security check.

We don't know what will transpire in the future, but we see a trend that is becoming more and more disturbing. If we can't afford to buy anything, money won't matter. We will need to share and to care. Love thy neighbour was not advice. It was a commandment spoken by Jesus Christ.

Chapter 19 – Chickens and Coop

Joel 2:26 And ye shall eat in plenty, and be satisfied, and praise the name of the Lord your God,

We thought long and hard about a type of poultry or farm animal that we could raise and would yield two types of food. The neighbors have sheep, so they have mutton and fresh sheep's milk. My husband did not forbid me, but he was not a fan of having chickens, particularly due to the smell, and the noise a rooster makes. We thought it would be good to have chickens for eggs and meat, as well as for the free fertilizer for the garden. I ordered the chicks, as there was a delay in being able to get them shipped, and then hurried to build the coop.

The chicken coop is something to think about for quite a while, before actually building it. Money can limit what you start with, compared to what you finally end up with. I wanted to build a coop with nesting boxes on the left and a coop with nesting boxes on the right, and a divided run with a walk-in door in the middle. That would have cost about $1,800, before this awful inflation kicked in. At today's prices, it would be about $3,500. I opted for the $900 version and that was not spent all at once.

I started out with only $200. As the build progressed, more was accomplished. Keep in mind that bigger is better in the long run. In my opinion coops sold in the farm supply stores will never be adequate, in terms of little coops at $400, unless you literally only want two chickens.

It is important to buy chicks from the hatchery. My first order from the hatchery was not great, due to my lack of knowledge. I ordered 10 chicks in a straight run thinking I would get one rooster, and I got five! That was impossible with the five hens. I felt like the hatchery packed the order with roosters to get rid of them. So, we gave away two. That meant ordering another 10, but all hens from a different hatchery. That was not a good experience either, as they didn't ship enough to fill the order. That meant another box would be shipped and they wanted to add "packing peanuts" as they call them, to ensure the missing chicks would arrive alive. That meant four extra chicks served as packing peanuts, and I had to argue that they must be hens, as I had too many roosters; that was the problem I was trying to solve. A few months ago one adult rooster died overnight for no visible reason. We now have 19 hens and two roosters (after giving two away), and it is perfect for about 15 to 19 eggs a day! That is enough for the neighbors, us, and our family. Recently, I let a broody mom hatch two baby chicks. She's in the sick bay with them and they are doing fine!

I read the stories a lot of backyard chicken owners wrote on the internet. The best advice ever was to put linoleum on the floor of the coop. I really find that easy to clean. Nesting boxes may be shared easily with the hens but they might have a favorite. We had three nesting boxes with a small board in front to keep the straw or pine chips from coming out. There is also a roosting bar right in front of the nesting boxes. Some kind of flap or door needs to be closed at night to prevent the chickens from sleeping/pooping in the nesting boxes. In the morning the nesting box door is opened and the hens can lay.

The current coop is 8 feet wide by 4 feet long and the roof peak is 6 feet high. It was built on sloping ground, so one end was blocked, and has black weed blocker under it. There is also an apron of hardware cloth buried along the outer edges, so no animals can dig in. The original run is 8 feet wide by 8 feet long and the roof peak is 6 feet high. The three nesting boxes are enough. The coop has a walk-in door that is 4 feet tall, and a 4-foot tall door out to the run. The main run has a 4-foot door out to the add-on run. All is enclosed with hardware cloth. The coop ceiling also has hardware cloth under the polycarbonate roof that sits on 1"x2" wood slats. This allows breathing space and airflow. I cut insulation board to slip in between the boards and roofing. It stays in, in the winter. In the summer, the insulation boards are taken out in certain places. The insulation board is not accessible to the chickens, as hardware cloth in the ceiling prevents that. Avoid drafts on the chickens. Ventilation is necessary above the roosting chickens, drilled or cut into walls covered with hardware cloth and with doors on hinges to close when needed in cold weather.

It isn't good to stoop down to go in and out of the coop or runs. I should have built at least a 5-foot high door in each case. I may make that alteration in the coming months. Mistakes are great teachers, as they are painful, costly and time consuming to correct. We built the four coop partitions and the floor on a flat area of the driveway, and then assembled them on location. I built the trusses in place. Treated wood is heavy, and after transporting the walls to the location, it was decided not the carry those trusses.

Over time, and from necessity, we have a "sick bay" and a "jail" LOL. The sick bay works for any chicken that needs to get better alone, and for babies that can't yet go in the run. They can see each other but not hurt each other. The jail was an add-on run area for roosters that were too aggressive, or a flock possibly endangering baby chicks that were integrating.

The pop-out door allows the chickens to go in and out to the run, and the bigger door can be kept closed, if it is windy or cold. Carabiners keep doors closed.

A really nice waterer that can be heated if you want, a good food feeder and tubs for water are important. The feeder I have needs a modification, as the chickens can scratch and dump all the food out. It must be filled a little bit each day. The area where they can access the food needs more partitions, so that their feet cannot get inside.

The new add-on run is 8 feet wide by 4 feet long and the roof peak is 6 feet high. I can separate the roosters if I want to, to give the girls a break. This area is referred to as the jail, and it is used if one of the roosters gets too rowdy with the girls or with the other rooster. It is a good place if one hen has baby chicks, to raise the babies before integrating with the rest of the flock. Most of the time the door is open and they all simply have more space to play.

I had the add-on run on one side, because it took less materials, instead of on the end and that was a mistake. So that meant tearing it all off and moving it board by board after a few months. It was not a fun process at all. The reason it was a failure was due to the water runoff from the coop roof onto the add-on. Putting the add-on on the end of the main run allowed me to extend the greenhouse plastic roof and the roof was made symmetrical at that point. Of course, two more trusses had to be built. I had to buy more hardware cloth, to line the roof and truss edge side. It also meant moving the door that was on the side of the original main run, to the far end going into the added-on run. I had to attach new hardware cloth in that main run where the old door opening was, in the side. That was a fun task. Sarcasm. It isn't so aggravating when you know it is a major improvement to life, but again, mistakes are really a lot of work. Water runoff is really a huge issue as the quantity of water is amazing and the weight of that water is shocking. Remember, no standing water can be allowed to accumulate on any roof.

The side of the original main run has a side plastic, so in the hot summer it gets rolled up and stapled, to let a breeze go through the run. It is put down in winter.

Bricks are lined up along the 2"x4"s in the inside on the ground. This keeps the chickens from pecking and digging holes to escape. I learned this trick from a man who wrote an article on the internet

regarding this problem. The bricks are only 59c each at the moment, if you buy them from a big box store. Chickens can move bricks, but not after they are embedded in dried mud in the ground.

Think about the chickens you want, as some are egg layers primarily, some are for meat, and some are dual purpose. When you order meat birds they cannot be all female and you get straight run which means there could be a quantity of roosters. If you order egg layers then you can choose all hens. If you choose straight run, you have no control over how many roosters you will get.

Our two roosters get along most of the year, but in spring they fight so they

must be separated for a period of time.

When ordering from the hatchery, you also can get a mix of breeds which means that you have small hens and huge roosters, possibly. The girls need saddles or capes to protect them from damage during mating.

If you plan to raise chickens, you will need to learn basic chicken vocabulary!

Chicks - baby chickens

Broody - when a hen wants to sit on eggs to hatch them

Brooder - heater to keep chicks warm, radiant heat is best, instead of the lightbulb

Comb - fleshy growth on top of head

Coop - safe place for chickens and it locks for the night

Nesting boxes - where hens lay eggs and 3 to 4 girls share each box

Roosting bars - where chickens sit to sleep or rest

Run - a place for chickens to run and play and it must have food and water

Hen - female chicken

Pullet - young female chicken

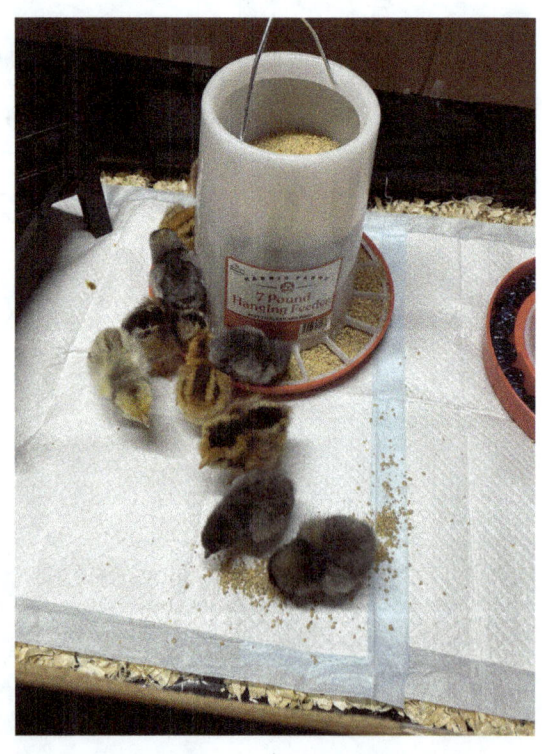

Rooster - male chicken

Cockerel - young male chicken

Straight run chicks - baby chicks that have not been sexed and this means you can get roosters with the hens

Scratch - corn or mixed grains

Starter feed - baby chick feed with or without antibiotics

Chicken feed - 18% to 20% protein feed for adult chickens

Bloom - the natural coating on eggs that you do not wash off if you want long-term storage protection on your eggs. Eggs with their bloom intact sitting on the counter can last up to a month, and kept in the fridge they can possibly last up to six months.

Egg basket - the wire basket for carrying eggs can be purchased in a smaller or larger size. The one shown can hold two dozen eggs without spills.

When buying chicks, you have the choice to vaccinate or not, so please research this topic. If you have a new batch of babies, the question is should you integrate these vaccinated babies in with the existing flock of adults that are not vaccinated.

Chickens like a construction sand dust bath, but not play sand for kids.

Keep a binder of information, and try to buy a few items for medical issues. We have not had many problems with our chickens because they are in an enclosed area. Some blue wound spray and antibiotic ointment without painkiller are good to have on hand.

Chapter 20 – Communication

Mark 13:33 Take ye heed, watch and pray: for ye know not when the time is.

Local, national, and international news will always be important to keep up with. Radios, TV channels, internet news, etc., are all great when the electricity and internet is functional.

> We are called to watch and pray. We cannot withdraw and hide. We are not to be timid. We responsibly watch and pray, but we don't obsess with negative news.

We also might need to broadcast our own news. In times of trouble, we might need to communicate with different locales.

If you have gone through a crisis, such as a destructive storm, you know that the cell phone towers go down, the internet fails and then nothing works. It isn't possible to call for help, buy groceries, charge gasoline or do banking without the technology. Wouldn't it be nice if you could communicate somehow?

In the days of old, CB radios and HAM radios were popular and are being increasingly more popular now, as people discover how fragile our communication technology is. It is not expensive to set up a basic CB radio and antenna, and it is important to have. If you think about the old military radios, they lasted for years and years and ran on tubes. Nowadays, the radios work with solid state. You can have a base station or a portable CB (Citizens Band) radio in your vehicle. Whatever choice you make, ensure that you have a safe power source. If it is a tube radio, make sure you have extra tubes and a tube tester.

The antenna has to be appropriate for your setup as well, and it needs to be high enough to send and receive signals from all directions, as well as have proper grounding against lightning strikes.

HAM amateur radio broadcasts can tell you what is going on around the world.

The short-wave radios or walkie-talkies are good for communications on the trail with each other, and many groups and militias use the UHF and VHF radios. They are affordable, but you do have to keep them charged up.

When the power goes out and we are using generators, we communicate with the CB radios. One of our family members might need medicine, a ride home, or we might need to share food or a can of gasoline, or borrow a tool, so communication is vital.

Learn the frequencies used, so you know which bands are primarily used for what type of communication.

CB Radio Frequencies

26,96500 – CB Channel 01 – open to all
26,97500 – CB Channel 02 – open to all
26,98500 – CB Channel 03 – open to all
27,00500 – CB Channel 04 – open to all – 4X4 Channel
27,01500 – CB Channel 05 -open to all
27,02500 – CB Channel 06 – open to all
27,03500 – CB Channel 07 – open to all
27,05500 – CB Channel 08 – open to all
27,06500 – CB Channel 09 – Emergency Communications
27,07500 – CB Channel 10 – open to all – Regional Roads
27,08500 – CB Channel 11 – open to all
27,10500 – CB Channel 12 – open to all
27,11500 – CB Channel 13 – open to all – Marine / RV
27,12500 – CB Channel 14 – open to all – Walkie Talkies
27,13500 – CB Channel 15 – open to all
27,15500 – CB Channel 16 – open to all - (also for SSB CB Radio)
27,16500 – CB Channel 17 – open to all – North / South Highway Traffic
27,17500 – CB Channel 18 – open to all
27,18500 – CB Channel 19 – Truckers – East / West Highway Traffic
27,20500 – CB Channel 20 – open to all
27,21500 – CB Channel 21 – open to all – Regional Roads
27,22500 – CB Channel 22 – open to all
27,25500 – CB Channel 23 -open to all
27,23500 – CB Channel 24 – open to all
27,24500 – CB Channel 25 – open to all
27,26500 – CB Channel 26 – open to all
27,27500 – CB Channel 27 – open to all
27,28500 – CB Channel 28 – open to all
27,29500 – CB Channel 29 – open to all
27,30500 – CB Channel 30 – open to all
27,31500 – CB Channel 31 – open to all
27,32500 – CB Channel 32 – open to all
27,33500 – CB Channel 33 – open to all
27,34500 – CB Channel 34 – open to all
27,35500 – CB Channel 35 – open to all
27,36500 – CB Channel 36 – open to all - (also SSB)
27,37500 – CB Channel 37 – open to all - (also SSB)
27,38500 – CB Channel 38 – open to all - (also SSB, LSB)
27,39500 – CB Channel 39 – open to all - (also SSB)
27,40500 – CB Channel 40 – open to all - (also SSB)

Chapter 21 – Sources of Income

Matthew 6:24 No man can serve two masters: for either he will hate the one, and love the other; or else he will hold to the one, and despise the other. Ye cannot serve God and mammon.

Full-time work, part-time work, sales of products, selling services, retirement, semi-retirement, and being an entrepreneur are all choices. What path would you take, to start? After a while, maybe you would become independent. Are you starting out young or retiring? Any phase of life is perfect for the forest escape. If I had known what I know now, I would have started out a lot younger! After having a lot of money, and having almost no money, we have experienced ups and downs throughout our 44-year marriage. At no point did money make us feel safe or content. However, in God's hands you feel both safe and content. Have faith and trust Him.

One thing is for sure, money never was all that important to us: God always made sure we could eat. Many life choices were made that seemed devastating at the moment, but God used each experience to show us His will and leading in our lives. When I quit my job to be a stay-at-home mom, my husband told me that God never let us starve. He said step out in faith. He was right and I never regretted leaving my career behind. I became an entrepreneur and never looked back. Both of our son's wives have been able to be stay-at-home moms for their children, too.

Love God more than money and you will be blessed. Our Father in Heaven can't give His children good gifts, if the children are too busy taking all that they greedily want. If you focus on God you will do what He wants you to do, instead of pursuing the almighty buck.

If you want to start your own business do your research and see what the needs are in the area you want to serve. Think about supply for materials, and shipping and profit margin. There are many platforms to sell on. If you sell online, you might end up giving away a little north of 13%. If you sell on some platforms, the fees are less. You can sell on local listings with many apps that do not charge fees and you can arrange safe meetings with people in public spaces to give them the products. You can sell fruits and vegetables in the farmer's market. There are craft fairs and many local events where you could make money. The internet provides a nice opportunity to sell nationally or even internationally if the shipping fees are not too high. If you have a service business, you can perform work for people in the area or have items shipped to you to work on. If you are really good at repairing tractors, ATVs, UTVs, cars or trucks, this is always in high demand. If you build furniture or kitchen cupboards, you could do that in your own shop. Whatever natural skill you were born with, coupled with the learned skills you have acquired in your career, you can use to make money!

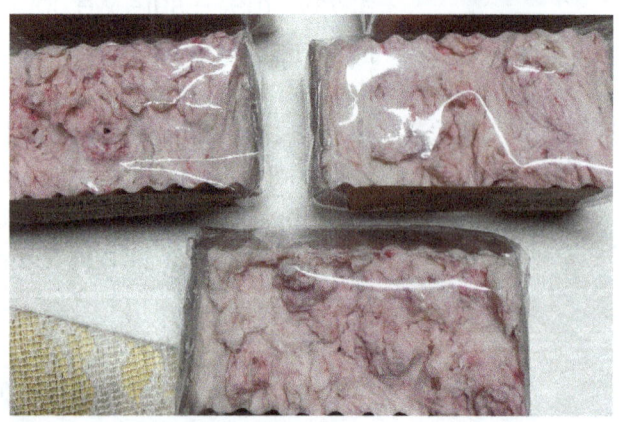

Make sure you know the laws for everything you want to do and have the utilities you need for your business or money-making activity before you buy your land.

Any hobbies that you like, such as making home-made soaps, crocheting, woodworking projects, fabric designing, ceramics, jewelry-making, woodburning, or sewing are all good way to make products to sell or use as gifts!

Chapter 21 - Sources of Income

Page 155

Think about your skills and your God-given gifts. What are you supposed to be doing in life? Should you be making Christian gifts, baking bread, writing books, or repairing equipment for everyone? Maybe you like lawn care and maintenance. If you repair cars, do bodywork, or like to restore old cars, this could be a way to generate income.

You don't necessarily have to earn money, to help out your financial situation. You could save money, by making home-made gifts. Everyone likes something home-made, as it becomes a sentimental possession.

Nowadays, you can use print on demand services and have a book printed to sell, or you can design fabric that can be sold by the yard on a platform. Greeting cards can be printed on glossy quality stock, with envelopes.

You can provide home office services for others, too, working on your computer.

Crafting is not only fun, but teaches us, our children, and our grandchildren how to do many different things. We don't know what we are good at doing, unless we try. We learn as we go and it's fun!

Chapter 21 - Sources of Income

Page 157

Chapter 22 – Sanitation

2 Corinthians 7:1 Having therefore these promises, dearly beloved, let us cleanse ourselves from all filthiness of the flesh and spirit, perfecting holiness in the fear of God.

If we make a lifestyle change, we will have cleaned up our lives, and taken ourselves out of a society that is in decline, out of a polluted city, or out of a neighborhood of poverty and violent crime. We want to feel clean and that we are doing the right things, in the eyes of God.

*Hebrews 11:7
By faith Noah, being warned of God of things not seen as yet, moved with fear, prepared an ark to the saving of his house; by the which he condemned the world, and became heir of the righteousness which is by faith.*

Practically, we have to think about keeping our forest escape clean. Personal hygiene, home cleanliness, flush toilets, composting toilets, and outhouses are a real concern. We can be making soap, bleaching, scrubbing and so much more to keep everything clean or sanitary.

The mindset of cleanliness will ensure that our homes, cooking areas, barns, coops and bodies will be reasonably clean and healthy. We want to limit germs so we don't get sick.

If we separate from the bad parts of society, we do not live in it and we are not subject to it. If we venture into society, we do what we want and need to do and then we hurry back home to peace and solitude. It is funny how we really change. We no longer want to be out and living the fast life, as we prefer the quiet of our home. It is our sanctuary.

You would want to stock up on things that will help you, such as hand sanitizer, soaps, bleach, surgical gloves, cleaning cloths, rubber gloves, and various cleaners for different surfaces. You would need laundry soap, dish soap, and disinfecting spray.

Clothes pins and a clothes line help with drying the laundry, and airing out blankets or brushing off rugs.

Buckets, dishpans, basins and hoses help you get water to where you need it for cleaning. Collecting rainwater in tubs can put water right where you need it.

Scrubbing is part of life. Scrub brushes are really good to have, in various sizes. The steel wool pads are also useful.

Lots of paper products including facial tissues, toilet paper and paper towels will make life convenient.

Garbage bags for trash, and zipper bags for food storage are vital.

Insecticides and insect repellents help you stay more germ free. The idea is to stay free from bites, stings or wounds, and free from infection. Learning to live this way, proactively avoiding injury and germs, will help you avoid leaving your home in times of chaos.

Especially if you have children or babies, diapers and wipes are vital, adhesive bandages, antibiotic cream, iodine, peroxide, and disinfecting bleach wipes for surfaces are all important.

Build up your cleaning supplies slowly over time.

Chapter 23 – Barter and Alliances

Lamentations 1:11 All her people sigh, they seek bread; they have given their pleasant things for meat to relieve the soul: see, O LORD, and consider; for I am become vile.

We may not always use money. When inflation is so high that we can't buy anything, money won't have any value anymore. A currency is only as good as its spending power. No one will want paper money because they need clean water or they need food, instead. Paper money won't feed you, if there is no store nearby or there is nothing in the store.

*Revelation 13:16-17
And he causeth all, both small and great, rich and poor, free and bond, to receive a mark in their right hand, or in their foreheads: 17 And that no man might buy or sell, save he that had the mark, or the name of the beast, or the number of his name.*

Imagine that our paper currency changes to digital. This is the way of the future, and it will usher in something almost unbelievable, until now. The digital currency could be monitored, and all transactions could be controlled. That isn't freedom. It would be government tyranny. We could be punished or controlled. Our assets could be frozen or taken. Will the chip go in the hand or forehead to be scanned? When the end times Mark of the Beast is implemented, we will not be able to buy or sell without that Mark. Will we be gone in the gathering to Jesus, or will we see the Mark of the Beast in our lifetime? That concept needs to be studied. Even if we are gone, what about those who are left behind?

Good business involves networking, and a homesteading lifestyle can be run like a business. We need alliances for tough times. We share out of love, but there will be needs and we may barter to survive.

Imagine, if a neighbor has potatoes they will trade for our eggs. They might have had a great crop of potatoes and can continue trading long term. We never run out of eggs, so this ensures that we have food. If we need a roof repair and the guy who is skilled at that needs his tractor repaired, we can do that. It is considered an even trade because both items are vital and we both would be thankful to have the repairs done. If one lady sews clothing and another is a baker, then they can barter back and forth and make a deal. We could trade seeds with each other, too.

If we teach the skills that have value, then our families can barter now and into the future. The skills of repairing and building are vital. What you raise or grow is a commodity to be traded with others. If you have bees, you can trade your honey for a portion of meat that a farmer has. If you are knitting mittens, knit an extra pair to trade. If you are sewing shirts, sew an extra one to trade. If you are good at mending clothing with holes in them, you can offer that as a service. If you can tomatoes, those can be traded for carrots someone has in their root cellar.

> **Your alliances can be through neighbors, family, friends, church, work, local organizations, farmers, stores, and more. Alliances are important for more than just bartering. It is important to have connections with village, state and government entities, to understand the news and issues in your area.**

If you buy supplies, buy a couple of extra things to use to trade with others. A couple of lighters could be traded for a dozen apples. Ammo could be traded for a good butcher knife. Extra kindling could be gathered and offered to the neighbor widow, in exchange for bread. If you know and love your neighbors, you know what they need. We are our brother's keeper, so we do prepare for their needs as well. This is being a good steward of what we have been given and what we have been blessed with.

We do not know what the future holds. Will we deal with sharp social decline? Will there be thieves? Will we be strong, if we are persecuted? If there is an enemy to fight, alliances would be helpful. Neighbors and family can keep watch. Others can patrol the land. The rest complete their tasks or take turns sleeping. Think spiritual warfare with demons that are using men and women on the ground.

Seasons change and needs change. Summer evenings you can crochet a blanket to trade in the winter. In the fall you are canning all of the fruits and vegetables to make it through the winter and you can trade with the neighbors. In the summer you are gathering wood for winter heat. Likewise, in the winter you are sewing summer clothes, starting seedlings indoors, and repairing things that will be used in the summer.

Some people are excellent hunters and gatherers, as well. The bounty they bring in can he bartered with. Venison can be traded for beef. Chickens can be traded for pork. If you have the skills to gather natural herbs, edible plants and mushrooms, these are valuable commodities. Foraging is an important skill. You can find wild garlic and wild onions. It is important to identify plants properly because some can make you sick, or are actually deadly.

Ethics are important when bartering. As Christians, it is important to believe that each trade is done in a way that your mother would be proud of. Imagine each trade with a stranger in your area is actually with your sister or your mom. You would want to be the best person you can be. We should never take advantage of each other. If a trade is a little unfair to your benefit, tell the person you are trading with that you owe them next time, and don't forget to give them something extra in the future.

Don't be ashamed to accept a gift from someone, when you are in need. Gifts from the heart, wanting nothing in exchange, are precious. We show gratitude with a big smile!

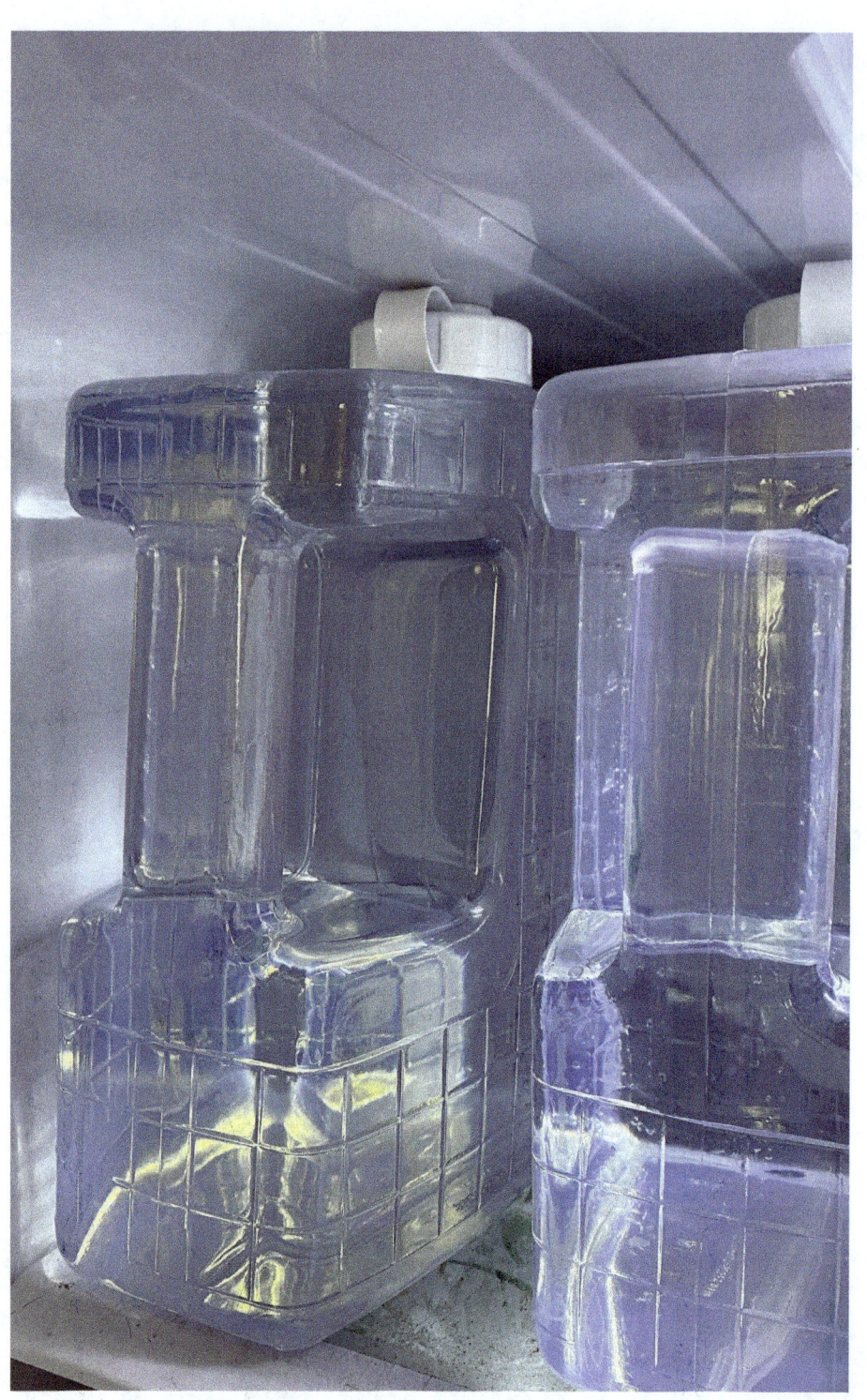

Chapter 24 – Sustainability

John 6:12 When they were filled, he said unto his disciples, Gather up the fragments that remain, that nothing be lost.

Reuse, recycle, upcycle, repurpose, etc., and be a good steward of God's blessings.

> **The more independent you become, the more nature-respecting your life will be.**

If you are filtering water, you are not buying plastic water bottles. You use pitchers of water. We recently made the change from buying jugs of spring water and cases of bottled water. Now, we just fill up pitchers in the fridge and our personal water bottles to carry around with us all day. We have another pitcher for filling up the coffee machine. That is a lot of plastic that is gone from our lives.

If you are using glass jars with rubber gasket lids, they are perfect for storing objects, so you are reusing something and not disposing of it. I keep my dried seeds in glass jars. I also save lard from cooking bacon and store that in glass jars in the fridge.

If you save your junk mail, you can be using it to start a fire in the winter. I open everything and save the regular paper - not the glossy paper - from the junk mail and wad it into a small ball. These are great for starting fires. I keep them in a box, and also in a bag hanging on the wall.

If you are independent you are not using gasoline to run to the store every minute. You want to have a list of things you need and what stores you will visit, in order, like making a big loop. Having "in days" and "out days" sets up a routine and you stop running out every single day for things. It saves time and money. Once a week for shopping is more than I actually want to do. I really don't like shopping. What I like less, is when I go to town and can't find what I need. The supply and demand issues are hitting us hard and literally nothing is in the store. You end up having to settle for something you don't want, or you pay so much more for it, just to bring it home. Some things are better just to get online and not waste the gasoline.

We use metal cans from the canned soup and canned vegetables for lots of things. They are great for sorting screws, nails, hardware, and all kinds of things, especially in the greenhouse! The metal cans, properly washed, can be used for all types of kid's crafts, too.

Think about maybe not being able to buy or to replace things with the volatile economy and exorbitant inflation. If you look around at what you have, it might be all you are ever going to have. How can you make it last longer? We probably would never throw anything out. It can be upcycled, repurposed and used for a much longer time.

Any packaging we get, we reuse when we need to ship something out. That includes, brown paper, bubble wrap, foam, padded sheets, and boxes. Everything I ship online comes from someone else's packing. That same packing is maybe going around the world to many other people, as many shippers do this same thing.

Whatever you have, make use of. Don't throw it away. Organize it. If you can't use it, someone else may trade you for it. I have plastic buckets from cat litter that are great for storing things. I can't use all of them, but some I have drilled holes in and planted onions or carrots. Some of the smaller types of containers would be great for storing used oil, lime, diatomaceous earth, or sand.

If your mindset is that you can't go buy more of anything, then you will use everything that you currently have to the best of your ability. You won't waste anything.

The vocabulary we encounter when speaking about not wasting anything is interesting, as follows:

Reuse
To reuse is to use again. If you have a container that held exterior screws, instead of throwing it away, use it again. Put various hardware items in it, such as screws, nails and bolts. We reuse the luncheon meat containers as they are now made like sealable containers you would buy. We put leftovers in them. Feed bags are also very useful.

Recycle
To recycle is to turn the plastic, cardboard, glass, or other, is to be (i.e.) melted down and made into something else in the future. We used to drop off cardboard for recycling, but we use it in the raised garden beds now.

Upcycle
To upcycle is to take something, such as a spaghetti sauce jar and improve it somehow, to use it for some other purpose. I keep my dishwasher tabs in a cleaned out spaghetti sauce jar. I plan to put rubber tape grips on the lid. The rubber seal keeps out moisture; it is easier to reseal than the zipper bags dishwasher tabs normally come in.

Repurpose
To repurpose is to take something that had an original purpose and use it for something new and different. If you have jeans that are all ripped out at the knees, you can make them into shorts. If you have big storage tubs and the lid got destroyed, you can use the tub in the garden to collect rainwater.

Borrow
To borrow is to not purchase. A friend shares their item with you, so you don't have to go buy it. If it is something you use once a year, it is crazy to spend money on it. We share the post driver or pounder. When you borrow, you must remember to return it promptly.

Reduce
To reduce is to not consume as much. If you reduce the number of trips to town, you save gasoline and money. If you use cloth grocery bags, you reduce how many plastic bags you use. Personally, I do both. I like the plastic bags to use as small garbage bags in the small wastebaskets. I use large cloth bags to consolidate three plastic bags, such as all bread items in one, and chips in another one. There are less trips in the house, when bringing in groceries. We use the insulated bags with ice packs for cold items.

Share

To share is to give a portion of yours to someone else. Seeds are a good example. The idea of having a homestead that is sustainable is really wonderful. In a good year, we could say it might be possible to perpetuate a way of life without much purchased from outside the homestead. To get to that point is tough.

> **An example would be a hyrdroponic system with fish. A fish tank generates waste and that in turn feeds the vegetables you are growing nearby. You have fish and you have vegetables and that system continues, as new fish are born and grow. Tilapia, catfish and trout are examples of the types of fish that can thrive in this environment.**

Another example is a flock of chickens that are raised for meat and eggs, as well as the added benefit of creating garden fertilizer from their droppings. It is self-perpetuating, because eggs hatch and more chickens are born. If they free range, it is basically free. If they are in a coop with an enclosed run, it is not cheap, as chicken feed is about $15 a bag. That lasts four days in summer with 21 chickens, if I also give them kale and scratch. In winter it lasts only three days, as they consume more to generate body heat.

Planting fruit trees is a good sustainable source of food. The trees produce food every year, as long as they are pruned properly and have fertilizer. We have one apple tree grown from a seed. It is slow at growing, only being about 18" tall, but it is still alive. We have two lemon trees and one is about 24" tall, so it is coming along nicely, considering it started as a seed the grandchildren planted.

The garden is self-perpetuating. Each year it gives food that can be used and preserved. Each plant also can have its seeds dried and kept for the next planting season. We have to be careful to use only non-GMO seeds in the garden. We do not want seeds with herbicides or insecticides built into them. We do not want babies in the womb to be consuming poison from the mother's food intake. We do not want unstable genetic changes in plants from one generation of plants to the next. In that way, the seeds will germinate in the spring. Grow healthy natural plants and save the seeds. You will not need to buy seeds each year. Share with friends and you will each have plants that you want in your garden.

Chapter 25 – Minimum Investment

Psalms 91:2 I will say of the Lord, He is my refuge and my fortress: my God; in him will I trust.

If you decide to make a lifestyle change and build your forest escape, imagine what would be basic and affordable to start. I have two scenarios that will help you think about the money and bare necessities to start out. If we choose to live simply and have only the basic necessities, it is not expensive. There is no mortgage. You will need a pickup truck, possibly a 4x4, depending on your property terrain.

Comfortable $40,000 to $45,000, and $400 monthly

If you buy 15 acres of land for around $30,000, it is probably the least you would want to buy for various reasons. If you get the deed in your name and pay payments over 10 years with financing from the seller, you could have a payment of $400 a month, if you put $2,000 cash down.

If your project is for one or two people, the cabin you build could be small to start – bedroom, living room, bathroom and kitchen – and it could be metal roofed/framed in/buttoned up for about $20,000, with the help of friends or hiring the Amish for the exterior, as we did.

Build in early summer so heat is not an immediate concern. Interior work can be done over time, but you need basics, so figure another $10,000 to have the bathroom and kitchen. Enjoy the process. You can always add on rooms, like an extra bedroom, pantry, or work room.

When winter finally comes, you will need a quality reliable wood stove, hearth, wall protection, and chimney for about $3,000 at a minimum. If you hook up electric and run basic plumbing, you will also need the septic system. Estimate about $5,000 for those luxuries!

Prioritize and build the things you can. You have drawn out your ideal homestead, and it has many things you can't afford initially. The fenced-in raised garden beds need to be built and filled with soil. Maybe the chicken coop and run need to be started, as well. You need basic tools, buckets, hoses, and spigots. Figure $3,000 to have the basics, and remember used items are great.

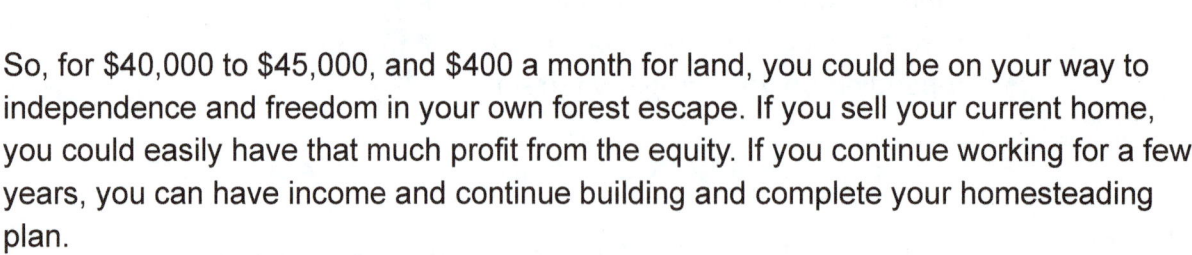

Stock your cupboards with water bottles, canned goods, and a good first aid kit, along with a fire extinguisher. Figure $1,000 for the emergency supply items.

So, for $40,000 to $45,000, and $400 a month for land, you could be on your way to independence and freedom in your own forest escape. If you sell your current home, you could easily have that much profit from the equity. If you continue working for a few years, you can have income and continue building and complete your homesteading plan.

If you live completely off grid, then some income source would be important until you have everything up and running properly. You can find materials people give away for free, let you pick up for free just to get rid of them, or have used for sale really cheap. You can repurpose things, too.

Minimum $12,500 to $14,000, and $200 monthly

> Let's say that budget has to be considerably less, to start. If you have $1,000 to put down on 5 acres of land, and payments of $200 per month are okay for five years, then the land is something you can get.

If you only have $10,000 for the small cabin, you could get a tiny house started, or you could buy or rent to own those little houses that they sell at storage building places. The one shown here is a screenshot of a local ranch style and the outright purchase price is around $10,000 for a bit bigger size on the web at 12 feet x 20 feet. You can rent an outhouse or use a composting toilet like the screenshot below. A good composting toilet is around $1,000 and there are many listed on the internet. A cheap chicken coop and small run could be built for $300. You would need a water solution. The lighting could be oil lanterns or LED indoors and solar-charging lights outdoors. At some point, you could add electric and sewer. If you want a garden, you  will need to fence it in with at least chicken wire, so posts and wire would be around $300. You can get a dependable small cook/heat wood stove like the screenshot shown and a chimney for $900 last I checked online. This forest escape solution is from $12,500 - $14,000 to start, with the monthly land payment of $200. You will still need the tools, paper goods and food, but you can start slow on accumulating things, or maybe you already have most of it. Just think camping and imagine a simple start. Long-term camping gets old in a hurry, so plan to make improvements.

Chapter 26 – Daily Routine

Genesis 2:15 And the LORD God took the man, and put him into the garden of Eden to dress it and to keep it.

We are meant to work. Homesteading is like the original job God gave us. He instructed us to dress and keep the garden of Eden. We work and we are able to eat. It is a simple concept. Nothing is for free.

Colossians 3:23-24
And whatsoever ye do,
do it heartily,
as to the Lord,
and not unto men;
24 Knowing that of the
Lord ye shall receive the
reward of the inheritance:
for ye serve
the Lord Christ.

Daily life is more efficient if there is a routine. Planning makes everything manageable, so you can accomplish more. We have differing routines by season. Changes need to be made as we grow older. To work smarter instead of harder is preferable.

The weather affects many things. Animal care is affected. It is nice on rainy days to do indoor chores, hand-crafted items, or conduct research online.

Some work is continual. Repairs for the home, storage building, greenhouse and coop, as well as maintenance of equipment really has to be handled throughout the year. Buying supplies will always be a monthly routine.

Spring

In spring, we have to plant seeds and get the heater going in the greenhouse. We have to prepare the garden beds, by hoeing and removing old debris, as well as treating the soil with fertilizers. We make a new batch of chicken fertilizer. We clean the yard, and cook food in the smoker. We are also concerned with channeling water runoff, and this year I had to make gravel steps to the greenhouse.

Summer

In early summer, we have the garden planted, cut wood for heating, find new water sources, maintain trails and roads, repair fences, cook on the BBQ grill, give extra water to the chickens, and add new ventilation to the coop.

Fall

In fall, we are canning foods, gathering kindling, splitting wood, weatherizing the doors to the house, ensuring there are no drafts in the coop, saving and drying the seeds from the garden plants, and making jerky, as well as stocking up the freezer for a possible rough winter.

Winter

In winter, we haul in wood, stack wood, make soups and chili, concentrate on maintenance of heating sources, get out salt buckets for ice, check maintenance of vehicles, and ensure the brooder/heaters are working properly, so if they need to be used they are ready.

In everything we do, we are acutely aware of the surroundings. At dawn, we see the sun starting to rise and the deer. We hear the birds singing and the squirrels chattering. We feel the moist morning fog, inhale fresh air, and enjoy the gentle breeze. We smell the flower blooms and the vegetables. Recently, in the garden, I ate the first strawberry and one of the first black raspberries. The taste was so sweet! This whole experience is energizing. When switching from winter to spring, we feel tired. The weather changes can be

harder on some people, than on others. I take extra B12 for energy.

My spring routine is not necessarily what your routine would be. I will give you an example. Chickens wake up at 3 AM, and I get up at 4 AM. I put the dog out/in; feed him and the cats. I work online from 5 AM to 7 AM. At 7 AM, I cut kale into small pieces and shred up some bread. When I first go into the chicken coop, I open the walk-out door and the pop-out door, so the chickens can go into the run. I throw the kale and bread. I open the nesting box door, so the hens can lay eggs. Next, the waterer and feeder are filled. I open the greenhouse windows/door, and water the plants. I water the garden. and do some weeding. I work online again from 8 AM to 10 AM. After that, I do household chores. Sometimes, I gather kindling. It is necessary to shovel the coop once a week and put new straw inside. I also put pine flakes in the nesting boxes. I always check my planner for projects and repairs that need to be done. We have some lunch, and more chores are done inside the home. I look at my online store on the platform, to see if I have sold anything. On rainy days, I try to make new items to sell. The garden needs daily care, feeding and watering. I take out the compost items from the kitchen to the compost bin. Supper is cooked and the chores are done. The chickens go back in the coop, the eggs are gathered, and the coop doors are closed. The greenhouse door is closed. It is time to rest. Each day is truly good.

ANNUAL PROJECTS

Quarterly

Jan / Feb / Mar	Apr / May / Jun
reload wood storage, creosote additive	cut fire wood, gather kindling
greenhouse started and heated	garden beds prepared and planted
coop insulation and heated	coop vents and airflow
extra blankets	summer clothing out; rain boots
repair tree damage	road maintenance, trails cleared
Q1	Q2

Monthly

Jan	Feb
bring in wood	creosot preventative
greenhouse cleaned out	plant potatoes, peppers, onions
coop straw, vents closed	run heater, shovel to beds
extra blankets out, space heaters	heavier clothes and socks
salt, clear ice	saw up fallen trees

Weekly

week 1	week 2	week 3
wood to deck storage	wood in to house rack	fill kindling box
stock pine	stock straw	stack unused planters
close vents	add straw in eaves	more straw in coop
heated blankets	space heaters	couch blankets
salt buckets and scoop	shovel to porch	straw on walkway

Chapter 26 - Daily Routine

Jul / Aug / Sept	Oct / Nov / Dec
split fire wood and stack	fire wood in house in rack/crates
fertilize, canning, 2nd planting broccoli	harvest seeds, hoe up dead plants
baby chicks, store up feed/scratch/straw	chicks laying, shovel coop to raised beds
more water for all	winter clothing out; winter boots
bush hogging	salt for ice, shovel, cover propane
Q3	Q4

Mar

- clear wood; sweep deck; get rid of bees
- plant seedlings
- start to open vents
- dress in layers, some hot days
- clear blocked roads

You can see the year broken into quarters, with goals to achieve. The breakdown is organized so that everything can be accomplished.

Start with annual goals and assign them to months. For the month's goals, assign them to weeks. In each week, you can see what you need to do.

week 4

- junk mail for starting fires
- empty old planters
- clear water ice
- supplemental heat
- salt steps

A spreadsheet is best on the computer, or you can use the front of your planner, where you can see the year at a glance. I use sticky notes there, because I can move them.

Chapter 26 - Daily Routine

Chapter 27 – Trust Jesus

Isaiah 1:18 Come now, and let us reason together, saith the Lord: though your sins be as scarlet, they shall be as white as snow; though they be red like crimson, they shall be as wool.

If you are a Christian who has repented of sin, believed Jesus Christ died for your personal sins, and asked Him into your heart as your personal Savior, you are saved. You are washed white as snow, so you can live this way moving forward. Don't look back at old sin and the old ways of your life. Don't let guilt of sin hold you back, or make you feel less confident. There is work to do for God. We can get busy.

John 3:17 For God sent not his Son into the world to condemn the world; but that the world through him might be saved.

Not only are you saved, but the Holy Spirit lives in you. Inside you. That means you are never alone. We can be brave.

God loves you. Love Him as a small child and trust Him as your Father in Heaven. Pray and ask Him what path you should take. Ask Him to lead your way. Pray and look for confirmation in any lifestyle change that you consider making. Don't do anything until you have the answers. Sometimes, the answer is slow, or the answer is no. We can be patient and obedient.

This is between you and God. Too many people look for social media approval or see what influencers say. Some people think too much about what haters say. We have to ignore all that. The social media throngs believe that the difference between right and wrong is how many people agree with them. God tells us what is right or wrong: it is not what popular opinion thinks. Popular opinion could take people to hell in a handbasket, and the sad thing is they won't even realize it! Don't be timid. Be brave. March forward boldly, as a born-again Christian, and pursue your dream whatever it may be. The path you follow will be the right one, if God is laying it out before you. We can see that the world is out of control for both those who are saved and those who are not saved. How we deal with the situation in the world is determined by our faith, or lack of it. As Christians we are in the world, but not OF the world. If we are too saturated in evil, we must separate from all the chaos and go to a place of peace. Jesus frequently went away from people, to a place of peace, to pray to His Father. In the forest escape we can worship and be separate, to have a quiet conversation with God. It is important to have a quiet place of solitude in nature. We can break free.

GOD LOVES US

God's loves us and wants to have a relationship with us. God wants us to love Him and minister to Him. Through grace and great love, God sacrificed His only Son. Jesus died on the cross as the sacrificial lamb for our sins past, present and future. Jesus came to save the world. We are the pearl of great price.

TRUST JESUS

Jesus lived in a way that provided a role model for us, showing us how to handle problems, how to worship, how to love our neighbors, and how to work. Jesus showed us how to love our Father in Heaven. In Revelation, Christ is revealed to us. End times events are revealed to us. In Matthew, Jesus told us not to worry, and that certain things must happen before He returns. Jesus not only spoke about things that are going to happen, but also the order that they will happen. If life is going to get tough, the tough better get going. Right? We must be spiritually strong, see with eyes that see, and hear with ears that hear. When other people suddenly realize they are in end times and are not prepared, at all, we will help them. We do not know how bad things will get in end times so we hope for the best, but plan for the worst. If we are gathered up to Christ, but friends, family, or neighbors are left behind, what we establish as a lifestyle now will help them survive until they become born-again saved Christians. Trust in the words Jesus spoke. Study the Bible.

> *Leviticus 20:26*
> *And ye shall be holy unto me: for I the LORD am holy, and have severed you from other people, that ye should be mine.*
>
> *1 Corinthians 3:11*
> *For other foundation can no man lay than that is laid, which is Jesus Christ.*

HOLY SPIRIT WITHIN US

The trinity refers to the three parts of God. God the Father, Jesus Christ the Son and the

Holy Spirit. Before Christ ascended to heaven, to the Father's right hand, He told us He would not leave us alone because God would provide a comforter. The comforter is the Holy Spirit and He lives within us. God speaks through the Holy Spirit, who guides and directs our lives in so many ways and enables us to use the gifts we have been given.

SHARING THE GOSPEL

We are free to serve, free to grow in faith and the knowledge of God, free to share the Gospel and free to live our lives in the manner Christ showed us. Jesus said to share the Gospel with other people. Jesus said the harvest is plentiful, but the laborers are few. We are called to be workers. The word Gospel means "good news". Many people in the world condemn and do not accept Christianity as good news. Many world organizations train us from childhood into adulthood to deny, mistrust and reject God's Word in the Bible. Satan is the leader of this deception and his job is to kill, steal and destroy. Even some Christians are not always sure of their true nature, abilities and position in life. Many Christians fall prey to Satan, and live a life without producing good fruit. That is why we must study the Bible daily. We must be free from distraction to listen to the Holy Spirit. God has a will for our lives, and we need to follow the path He sets out before us.

Chapter 28 – God Answers Prayer

2 Chronicles 7:14 If my people, which are called by my name, shall humble themselves, and pray, and seek my face, and turn from their wicked ways; then will I hear from heaven, and will forgive their sin, and will heal their land.

Always remember God answers prayer, and thank Him.

When we struggle, we pray and ask for God's help. After, when things are going great, we forget how many times God answers our prayers. If we document each prayer and each answer to prayer, we will always remember how many times God has blessed us. A prayer journal is really important. We don't always get an immediate answer to prayers. Sometimes, God answers in his time, or not at all. It is important for us to realize that all is in God's timing, and we only want to do what is according to His will. An answer to prayer at a later time, is the perfect time. No answer to the prayer means that we shouldn't move ahead. No confirmation to what we feel is an answer to prayer also means not to proceed. Pray about lifestyle choices. Ask God what you should do.

When we chose this path, we prayed and we looked for confirmation. We decided to pursue our forest escape and put our home for sale. We sold our home in NY in two weeks. That was shocking! We needed affordable land on payments. We called about land, and we mentioned that we wanted to ask the Amish to build us a small cabin. The man on the other end of the phone call said he was indeed an Amish man. Furthermore, he agreed to sell the land with owner financing, over 10 years. This was one form of confirmation. The Amish contractors did build the exterior of the cabin. All throughout the process we had blessing after blessing, along with struggle after struggle. The victories were much more sweet after a time of trouble. The chosen path is not easy, but God's blessing is ever-present. Our cabin in the woods was built by love. Our family helped in all aspects and everyone has taken a turn living in this cabin in the forest, during changes in their lifestyles that they pursued nationally and internationally. It was imparted to me that the whole family would enjoy living in this home before any of it happened. It feels miraculous. God's grace made all of this possible. We can say for certain that it all was meant to be, and there is so much more that we don't even know about yet, in the future. In the end times, I believe this cabin in the woods will be used for much more.

It is a burden on my heart that people never forget all the good things God has given them. I felt so much guilt whenever I moved on and forgot a really wonderful blessing. Each day, I say hello to God: I'm here. I want to thank God for each blessing, daily. He is always with us and loves us. We must have a personal relationship with our Father in Heaven. How sad to forget Him, or to not say thank you. We breathe this day because God wills it. Tomorrow we may not be here. Will people remember each of us as someone who loved God, and encouraged others to love Him and learn about Him?

God speaks daily.

Are you listening?

Are you writing down the many blessings
that God shows you daily?
Are you journaling the main points that the Holy Spirit reveals
in deep prayer?

Are you motivated to act
on those revelations and blessings?

It is time to use our gifts and to do God's work!

*We celebrate our Savior's birth in many ways.
The cabin Christmas tree is a special blessing.
The tree is from God, so lovely, and the aroma from the pine is heavenly.
There is history in decorating the tree and my tears always fall, remembering the past,
as the ornaments are very old, handed down from generation to generation.
The children make ornaments and crosses, and are joyful decorating each year.
The dark room in the evening with only the tree lights on
exudes an ambiance of peace and love.
The star of our Savior shines brightly in the dark.*

Chapter 29 – Future Hope

Revelation 3:14-22 And unto the angel of the church of the Laodiceans write; These things saith the Amen, the faithful and true witness, the beginning of the creation of God; 15 I know thy works, that thou art neither cold nor hot: I would thou wert cold or hot. 16 So then because thou art lukewarm, and neither cold nor hot, I will spue thee out of my mouth. 17 Because thou sayest, I am rich, and increased with goods, and have need of nothing; and knowest not that thou art wretched, and miserable, and poor, and blind, and naked: 18 I counsel thee to buy of me gold tried in the fire, that thou mayest be rich; and white raiment, that thou mayest be clothed, and that the shame of thy nakedness do not appear; and anoint thine eyes with eyesalve, that thou mayest see. 19 As many as I love, I rebuke and chasten: be zealous therefore, and repent. 20 Behold, I stand at the door, and knock: if any man hear my voice, and open the door, I will come in to him, and will sup with him, and he with me. 21 To him that overcometh will I grant to sit with me in my throne, even as I also overcame, and am set down with my Father in his throne.
22 He that hath an ear, let him hear what the Spirit saith unto the churches.

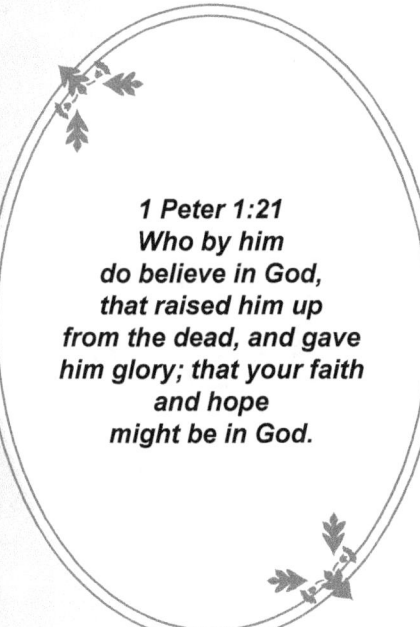

1 Peter 1:21
Who by him do believe in God, that raised him up from the dead, and gave him glory; that your faith and hope might be in God.

Let that Scripture sink in. Do you think that the Laodicean church describes our church age today? Does Jesus want to figuratively spew us out of His mouth? Originally. Jesus spoke of a Christian assembly or congregation. This was contrary to the synagogues with aggressive political behavior, and contrary to the churchianity of today that can be exclusionary. How many churches cater to the ones with money so that the tithes keep flowing? What about the one who tithes a penny or a dollar, or perhaps cannot tithe at all. Where is the outreach to them? Where is the first love? The love of Jesus should be first and foremost.

It is my observation that modern society predominantly either does not talk about God, persecutes Christians, blasphemes God, or produces weak Christians who have little faith and no skills to live through end times. We see the effects of departing from God are devastating, marriages suffer, and the children are wandering around lost. The churches have pastors that preach so people feel comfy and will tithe more money. Pastors have been committing crimes. Violence is increasing. People are angry, anxious, and depressed. It is all falling apart. The fabric of society is falling apart. The church is falling apart. The family is falling apart. I feel that we cannot look to society, or any role model in it, to provide hope.

So, we separate from society's ways and we turn to God if we want to break free. We study on our own, letting the Holy Spirit be our pastor. We withdraw from a shallow church. We tend to study every single day, being close to God, instead of once a week because it is all we can tolerate at a church that forgot its first love. Worship is about love for Christ and not about love of church, or love of an office in church.

If we are not hurting - if we are comfortable - we rarely think about God. He allows hurt to come into our lives, to bring us back to Him. Would it not be easier, to turn to Him in everything, instead of waiting for that grievous pain to bring us back?

Hope is in God. We have to change our lives to revolve around Him and for Him. God needs us to minister to Him. God wants us to love Him. Jesus paid the price for our sins, and we should not waste our lives. Our lives are for His purpose. We are the pearl of great price. We are the remnant, and we are called to be the overcomers.

We also see finger pointers saying one thing is wrong or another thing is wrong, and in the end there is nothing enjoyable to do at all, because it has been condemned by man. One judges to feel superior, but in the end all are sinners and none are better than others. Exposing hidden sin in the end shows us this many times. We should reason together, pray for each other, and help someone who repents of sin. If we approach

all in love, then people grow instead of hate. Enjoy life as God leads you. If you believe something is good and God approves, then enjoy. Just like social media, we cannot allow others to tell us what is approved. We must think for ourselves. Those who walk around judging don't have a life. They need to look in the mirror to see what they can improve about themselves and quit micromanaging others. We can point out Scripture to help our brothers and sisters in Christ, to help them in love. There are too many Christians taking away joy from other Christians, and stealing their hope. With that said, we shouldn't allow people to have that power. God gives all hope, and Jesus opens doors that none may shut. Don't allow anyone to take away your joy.

We can live a productive life, doing exactly what God asks of us, and be

exactly where He wants us. We have gifts from God and need to get busy. We cannot do these things for God, mixed in with the bombardment of evil that society not only allows, but encourages. We must be separate as much as possible, so we are healthy and have healthy relationships.

We must trust that God wants good things for us, and that He is watching over us, in good times and in bad.

If we concentrate on the wonderful world that God has made, we see wildlife everywhere in a forest escape. We see lizards, frogs, butterflies, flowers, deer, rabbits, turkeys, and many species of trees and birds. All of creation is wonderful and beautiful. It is made by God's hand, so it is perfect. We should be able to get up early in the morning, step out into the dawn's early light and feel the cool mist of the air. We should hear the birds singing after a rain. We should hear and enjoy the peepers peeping in the evening. We should see the stars and the moon in the night sky. All of this is free to enjoy. It just requires moments of solitude to ponder all that God has given us.

> We should feel small, so that we can see our great God.

If you grow flowers, you see a miracle from a seed or bulb grow and bloom. It is a small but mighty thing. I love seeing this process. It is incredible beauty!

Wildlife is all around and God made so many wonderful creatures to watch and protect if need be. Nature should inspire a person to think about God's creation. It should make us feel closer to Him.

When we are busy, we think less and worry less. Most people think too much and get depressed. Be thankful and work hard at something. In homesteading life you won't have time to be depressed or anxious. We notice all the small blessings that cheer us up. Morning chores are started with noticing that the lilies are blooming. We smile!

How does a person live each day, having great hope? We know God loves us and Jesus is coming back, first of all. We also know not to be troubled because Jesus says not to be troubled, because certain things must happen first. Study the Sermon on the Mount. Be separate living in the world, and not of the world. Next, we know the Holy Spirit lives in us, if we are born again Christians, so that means we are never alone and will be guided every step of the way. We have to listen to the still small voice of the Holy Spirit. Last, we must convert and be like a small child. Faith is trusting God without seeing the proof beforehand. If we can go through each day remembering these points we won't feel despair, and we will have the energy to do the work for the Lord. So, start each day studying the Word of God in the Bible and let Scripture be revealed by the Holy Spirit. Consider these verses of Scripture:

2 Corinthians 6:17-18 Wherefore come out from among them, and be ye separate, saith the Lord, and touch not the unclean thing; and I will receive you, And will be a Father unto you, and ye shall be my sons and daughters, saith the Lord Almighty.

John 3:16-17 For God so loved the world, that he gave his only begotten Son, that whosoever believeth in him should not perish, but have everlasting life. For God sent not his Son into the world to condemn the world; but that the world through him might be saved.

1 Thessalonians 4:16 For the Lord himself shall descend from heaven with a shout, with the voice of the archangel, and with the trump of God: and the dead in Christ shall rise first:

Matthew 24:6 And ye shall hear of wars and rumours of wars: see that ye be not troubled: for all these things must come to pass, but the end is not yet.

1 Corinthians 6:19 What? know ye not that your body is the temple of the Holy Ghost which is in you, which ye have of God, and ye are not your own?

Matthew 18:3 And said, Verily I say unto you, Except ye be converted, and become as little children, ye shall not enter into the kingdom of heaven.

Mark 11:22 And Jesus answering saith unto them, Have faith in God.

1 Corinthians 6:20 For ye are bought with a price: therefore glorify God in your body, and in your spirit, which are God's.

Colossians 3:23-24 And whatsoever ye do, do it heartily, as to the Lord, and not unto men; 24 Knowing that of the Lord ye shall receive the reward of the inheritance: for ye serve the Lord Christ.

2 Timothy 2:15 Study to shew thyself approved unto God, a workman that needeth not to be ashamed, rightly dividing the word of truth.

When you see someone feeling down, help them see the good in life. Help them commit to seeing God's will for their life. Help them study God's Word.

Help those people see the gifts God has given them. Don't let them fade away and give up. Inspire those around you.

Be the light that shines in the dark.

Now is the time to have that energy to prepare, to have a new lifestyle, to quit playing the games society wants you to play, and now is the time to stop saturating yourself with the evil in the world. Stop social media if it is overwhelming: I deleted most of my accounts. Stop watching TV just for the sake of watching something. Limit the news you take in so that it is not making you depressed. Know what is going on but don't be saturated with it. Watch and pray. Stress and stress relief.

Working outdoors, learning new things, sharing new experiences with others, and feeling vulnerable in a new situation will all help you to be humble, to ask questions, and to become closer to God.

What are we made of? Are we able to do great things? Most of the time, no. But with God's help, we can do anything and everything He wants us to do! The fear of following a path that we have no idea where it goes melts away and it becomes exciting! Find out what you are made of. Can you learn, try repeatedly, fail miserably, try again, and keep working until it hurts? Find out what type of person you are and will become with God's leading, guidance and strength! You will surprise yourself and see the divine hand of God reach out and touch you. Everyone should have an opportunity like this.

It is my sincere wish that sharing all of this journey will help you, as the reader, and inspire you to break free from the chains we all impose upon ourselves. Looking back many times, if we could have seen past our own point of view with another perspective, we might have lived differently. If we are not afraid, and trust God completely, we will live life more fully. If we obey Jesus, and love ourselves, our Father in Heaven, and our neighbors, the world would become a better place.

God bless you!

Mark 10:15 Verily I say unto you, Whosoever shall not receive the kingdom of God as a little child, he shall not enter therein.

Titus 2:11-14 For the grace of God that bringeth salvation hath appeared to all men, Teaching us that, denying ungodliness and worldly lusts, we should live soberly, righteously, and godly, in this present world; Looking for that blessed hope, and the glorious appearing of the great God and our Saviour Jesus Christ; Who gave himself for us, that he might redeem us from all iniquity, and purify unto himself a peculiar people, zealous of good works.

John 14:15-17 If ye love me, keep my commandments. And I will pray the Father, and he shall give you another Comforter, that he may abide with you for ever; Even the Spirit of truth; whom the world cannot receive, because it seeth him not, neither knoweth him: but ye know him; for he dwelleth with you, and shall be in you.

Matthew 28:19-20 Go ye therefore, and teach all nations, baptizing them in the name of the Father, and of the Son, and of the Holy Ghost: Teaching them to observe all things whatsoever I have commanded you: and, lo, I am with you alway, even unto the end of the world. Amen.

Jeremiah 1:5-8 Before I formed thee in the belly I knew thee; and before thou camest forth out of the womb I sanctified thee, and I ordained thee a prophet unto the nations. 6 Then said I, Ah, Lord GOD! behold, I cannot speak: for I am a child. 7 But the LORD said unto me, Say not, I am a child: for thou shalt go to all that I shall send thee, and whatsoever I command thee thou shalt speak. 8 Be not afraid of their faces: for I am with thee to deliver thee, saith the LORD.

1 Timothy 2:1-6 I exhort therefore, that, first of all, supplications, prayers, intercessions, and giving of thanks, be made for all men; 2 For kings, and for all that are in authority; that we may lead a quiet and peaceable life in all godliness and honesty. 3 For this is good and acceptable in the sight of God our Saviour; 4 Who will have all men to be saved, and to come unto the knowledge of the truth. 5 For there is one God, and one mediator between God and men, the man Christ Jesus; 6 Who gave himself a ransom for all, to be testified in due time.

www.ingramcontent.com/pod-product-compliance
Lightning Source LLC
Chambersburg PA
CBHW060420010526
44118CB00017B/2299